CW00543585

ARNE & CARLOS

30 SLIPPERS
TO KNIT AND FELT

Fabulous projects you can make, wear and share

Search Press

First published in Great Britain in 2015
by Search Press Limited
Wellwood, North Farm Road,
Tunbridge Wells, Kent TN2 3DR

Also published in the United States of America
in 2015 by
Trafalgar Square Books
North Pomfret, Vermont 05053

Originally published in Norwegian as
30 tøfler, ett Grunnmønster

Thank you to Laila Kristin Willgunnsdottir Bøhle for helping us to develop and test the slipper soles. Many thanks to the world's best pompom maker: my mother, Carmen Zachrison, who made so many wonderful pompoms for this book!

ISBN: 978-1-78221-352-9

Translation: Carol Huebscher Rhoades
Photography: Ragnar Hartvig
Stylist: Ingrid Skansaar
Charts: Arne & Carlos
Book Design: Lise Mosveen (www.mosveen.no)
Models: Guro Strande, Arne & Carlos

Printed in China

10 9 8 7 6 5 4 3 2 1

Contents

Preface

As the years go by, we find ourselves appreciating more home comforts, whether we live in a house, apartment, or cottage, or on a boat. For us, nothing says comfy more than a pair of lovely, colorful, soft, warm slippers! We always pack our slippers when we are preparing for one of our long trips around the world. When we get to the hotel room, we put on our favorite slippers and relax to get ready for the next day. Longing for home disappears as soon as we are wearing our little reminders of Tonsåsen, Norway, where we live.

Slippers are a sign of a more settled life at home in a comfortable environment where we are not stressed. It's important for us to enjoy our time at home—and our slippers contribute to that.

Slippers are fun to make, wear, and share with others. When you are young, soft, comfy gifts are perhaps not the most popular, but the day comes when those presents don't arrive, and then you realize that they were perhaps the best gifts you had ever gotten. Someone has thought well of you and taken the time to knit slippers so you can enjoy warm and cozy feet. There is a lot of comfort in slippers.

There is always something distinctive each time you felt slippers—and it's exciting to see what will come out of the machine. What happened this time? Are they the right size? It is exciting to see the difference between a knitted-in pattern and one embroidered on with duplicate stitch. Whenever we see the results of a pair of slippers, we want to make more.

In this book, we have designed slippers inspired by our own universe. Christmas and our garden are obvious enough and a slipper book without rabbits is just not a proper slipper book!

So, get your needles and yarn, curl up in a comfy chair, and enjoy the good times!

Arne & Carlos

Chapter 1

INTRODUCTION

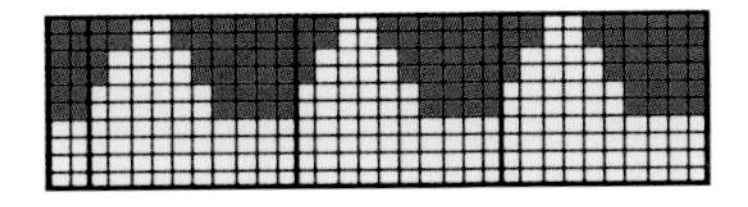

Many years ago, we knitted some slippers from a pattern we found in an old weekly magazine. They were worked back and forth and sewn together before being felted. The size was right but they quickly wore out. We got the old pattern back out and started knitting the three sizes given and then we knitted the same sizes our own way: knitted like socks with two strands of yarn that we alternated every stitch, almost like two-end (twined) knitting.

By knitting with two strands, we made the slippers thicker and less elastic than those knitted back and forth. Whether we knitted in a color pattern or with two strands of a single color, the slippers were the same thickness. Even when the sizes of slippers knitted in different techniques were the same, we felted them more.

When we shaped the toes on four needles as for a hat (or a Christmas ball), the slippers were rounder at the tip, similar to the old slippers that we knitted back and forth. So, when you knit these slippers, it will be like knitting a large sock, except for the toe; you might think something is wrong when you get there because it's not shaped like a regular sock.

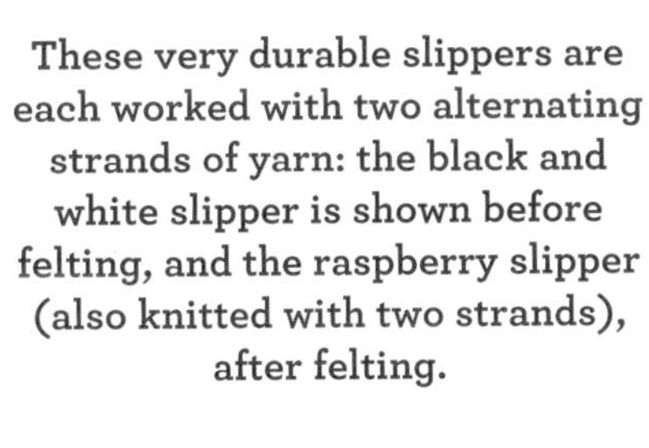

These very durable slippers are each worked with two alternating strands of yarn: the black and white slipper is shown before felting, and the raspberry slipper (also knitted with two strands), after felting.

The man with the pink crochet work was photographed in France in 1906.

Men who knit

Our slippers were inspired by sock knitting, and it's time to speak up for the men who have knitted throughout time. In the old days, it was common for men to knit, as you can see in the painting *Shepherd on the Heath*, painted by Frederik Vermehren (1855), which today hangs in the National Gallery of Denmark in Copenhagen. Knitting and animal herding go well together—as Arne knows, since he spent summers in the mountains and watched the cows. Because there were many free hours in the pasture before the cows returned home in the evening, that time could be used for knitting and crochet. "Only lazy people sit with their hands in their lap," his grandmother always said...

The people who lived there were very strange. Their clothing was poor, their kitchen utensils very basic. But I knew that those who lived on the heath lands often kept precious metals in an unpainted chest or in an untidy clothes cupboard, as well as a thick notebook inside a patched sweater. So, for that reason, when my eye—as soon as I stepped in—fell on an alcove, totally stuffed with stockings, I correctly guessed that I found myself in the house of a well-off stocking peddler (it should be said within parentheses that I've never known a poor one).

Steen Steensen Blicher: *Stories from the Heath Lands,* **"The Stocking Closet"**

REGIA
Latex

Chapter 2

MATERIALS

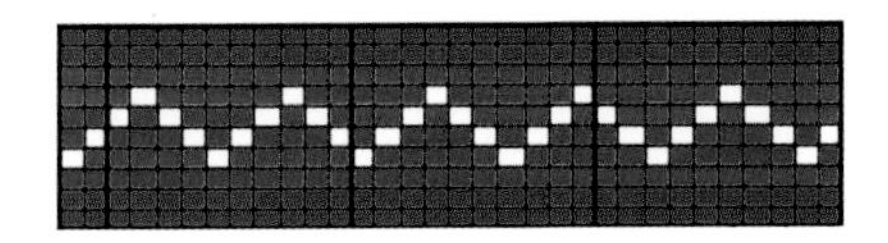

YARN THAT FELTS WELL: We used Rauma's Vamsegarn (CYCA #4, worsted/afghan/aran; 100% wool; 91 yd/83 m / 50 g), but there are other sources for durable yarn—for example, Fritidsgarn from Sandnesgarn. It is important to keep in mind that different yarns felt differently. We recommend that you knit and test one slipper first so that you can be absolutely sure that the yarn you've chosen will yield the same results as the yarn in the patterns.

YARN FOR CROCHETING THE FLOWERS AND FRINGE: We used Mitu from Rauma, which is available in a good color range, but you can substitute other yarns suitable for the same size crochet hook. Mitu is a DK/light worsted weight yarn (CYCA #3); 50% alpaca, 50% wool; 109 yd/100 m / 50 g.

YARN FOR EMBROIDERY: We embroidered the cross stitch patterns with DMC Mouliné Stranded Cotton (117), 100% cotton, 6 strands. We embroidered duplicate stitch motifs with Vamsegarn, the same yarn as for the knitting.

NEEDLES: 16 in / 40 cm circular, U.S. sizes 8-10 / 5-6 mm.

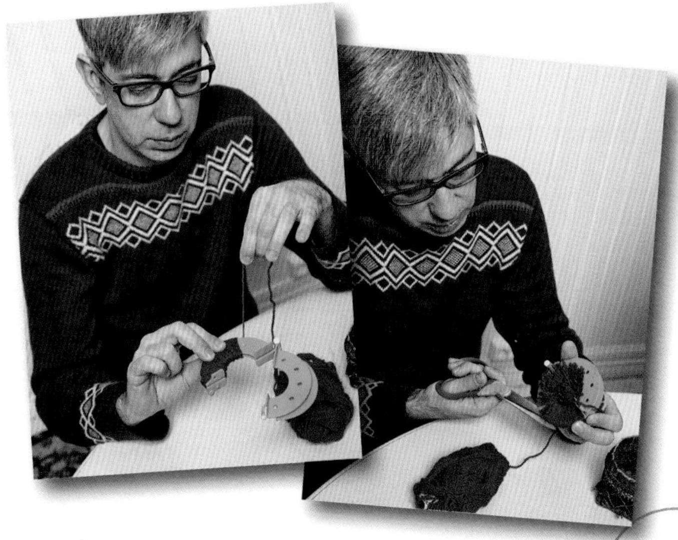

CROCHET HOOKS: U.S. sizes D-3 and E-4 / 3 and 3.5 mm and between H-8 and J-10 / 5 and 6 mm.

SEWING AND TAPESTRY NEEDLES

WASTE CANVAS: We used Aida waste canvas (#352) with 32 holes per 4 in / 10 cm, which you can usually purchase in yarn and sewing shops.

KNITTING MILL: We bought our 4 in / 10 cm knitting mill at a Panduro craft store in Norway. Check online and local craft and hobby stores for availability.

BEADS: You can find beads in sewing, bead, and yarn stores or craft shops.

FOR FELTING: You will need some slippery soap such as green soap, Milo or grated Ivory Soap bars. If you want to felt by hand, we recommend that you obtain a washing board, and if you really want to go professional, find a felting board. We like to keep it simple and felt in the washing machine.

MAKING POMPOMS: You can construct a pompom maker by cutting out two circles in cardstock in the desired diameter, or you can buy pompom makers in various diameters. We bought our pompom maker (item #10871) at Du Store Alpakka but you can also find a variety of sizes made by Clover. We used the 3½ in / 9 cm size for the larger pompoms and the 2¼ in / 5.5 cm one for the little ones. Even if you make them on the same size pompom maker, pompoms will be slightly different sizes when they are finished, as you will usually trim them to make them as round as possible. If you are making several, make them at the same time so they'll be as similar as possible.

Decorative Bands and Loops: We used traditional Norwegian sweater bands for our decorative bands and loops. You can find a good selection of these at knitting shops around Norway or at Scandinavian craft shops in other countries.

Liquid Latex for the Soles: This is highly recommended so that you don't slip on a smooth floor in your newly felted slippers. Luckily, you can give your slippers an anti-slip treatment. You can buy Liquid Latex at hobby shops. It comes in a bottle with a large opening so you can pour it on and cover the sole completely. It dries in a few hours. You can also use Regia ABS Latex from Coats, which is fun to apply because you can apply it in various patterns on the sole and you don't need to cover the sole completely.

So we had finally done all the measuring and had everything gathered together. We had our yarn ends over the hook in the ceiling above the table and had also begun to put the 5 needles to work. Then the schoolmaster said: "If any of you wants to sing or tell a story, it will be fine while you do these things."

The townships of Lysgård and Hammerum had developed long ago from the so-called knitting cottages. These were the places for knitting stockings, socks, and other items of knitwear that helped earn the cash necessary for rent, fees, etc. Niels and Steen Blicher described the "knitting cottages" in their survey, pointing out the advantages of this type of work: The participants saved light (!), they had competitions to see who could finish first, and were all gladdened by this collective entertainment.

Steen Steensen Blicher, *Stories from the Heath Lands*, "Knitting Cottages"

Safety is important! Make flowers, stars, or circles out of liquid latex on the slipper soles to walk safely on smooth floors.

The two larger slippers were knitted with Rauma Vamsegarn; the gray slipper is size Small and the patterned slipper is size Medium. The Small size's length from heel to toe is 9 in / 23 cm. For the Medium size, the length from heel to toe is 10¾ in / 27 cm. The Small slippers are knitted with the same pattern and needles in Schachenmayr's yarn for felting, Wash+Filz-It!. Wash+Filz-It! is a soft yarn that felts well and, if you want to make child-size slippers, this would be a good yarn choice. Knit a sample and test it in your washing machine.

ABBREVIATIONS

ch	chain
cm	centimeter(s)
CO	cast on
dc	double crochet (= British treble crochet)
in	inch(es)
inc	increase
k	knit
k2tog	knit 2 together
LLI	left lifted increase—knit st on needle and then knit into left side of st below the one just knitted
mm	millimeter(s)
p	purl
p2tog	purl 2 together
pm	place marker
rem	remain(s)(ing)
RLI	right lifted increase—knit into right side of st below that on needle and then knit st on needle
rnd(s)	round(s)
RS	right side
sc	single crochet (= British double crochet)
sl	slip
ssk	slip, slip, knit—slip 1 knitwise, slip 1 knitwise, knit together through back loops
st(s)	stitch(es)
tr	treble (= British double treble)
WS	wrong side
yo	yarnover

Chapter 3

BASIC SLIPPERS

We have developed three basic patterns for our slippers: 1) "clog" slippers without a cuff, 2) slippers with longer cuffs, and 3) slippers with shorter cuffs. The beginning for each type of slipper is different, but once you get to the heel they are all the same.

SIZING

The sizes can vary a lot depending on what type of washing machine you use. The water quality, knitting gauge, and how much you have in the machine all affect the felting process. Even the colors can be significant—we have observed that some colors felt better than others. In our washer, slippers knitted with gray yarn felt more than those worked with purple yarn.

Finally, and after much testing, we determined the sizing as follows:

Small (S): U.S. women's sizes 4-7½ / European sizes 34-38
Medium (M): U.S. women's sizes 8-11; men's 6-9 / European sizes 38-42
Large (L): U.S. men's sizes 9-13 / European sizes 42-46

However, this is not an exact science, and many things can happen during the process. If the slippers are much too big when you remove them from the washer, you can put them through another cycle, and they will, in all likelihood, felt more. If the slippers are too small, you can wear them and stretch them out while they are still wet.

It is important that you felt the slippers in the washer with something else so that they get a little "beating." We've tried a large bath towel, some washrags, and some of our dog Freja's rubber balls. It is also important that you don't fill the washer with too many things—a bath towel and two rubber balls are more than enough.

KNITTING GAUGE IS IMPORTANT!

There are often problems with knitting gauge. Many knitters don't check it and then are disappointed when the finished piece does not come out as expected. To avoid this problem, we highly recommend that you knit a gauge swatch that will be large enough for you to check the gauge—4 in / 10 cm across. For Rauma Vamsegarn, the recommended gauge is 14-16 sts in 4 in / 10 cm when knitted with needles U.S. 8-10 / 5-6 mm. We prefer a gauge of 16 sts in 4 in / 10 cm with this yarn. We both knit rather tightly and have to use needles U.S. size 10 / 6 mm to get the right number of stitches in 4 in / 10 cm. We have met lots of knitters and know that most knit more loosely than we do. If you are one of them, try out your gauge swatch with U.S. 8 / 5 mm needles.

Basic Slippers

S (M) L

Knit the basic slipper in the size closest to your shoe size and try the slipper on when you work the rounds/length for the foot. Put the unfinished slipper on, put your heel at the very back of the slipper and check to make sure the piece reaches the tip of your big toe. Now you are ready to begin the toe shaping.

CASTING ON FOR THE FIRST ROUND:

Photo 1: Cast on with the long-tail method using 1 strand of yarn and a short circular or 5 dpn U.S. size 8-10 / 5-6 mm. If you only need a small amount of one color, bring out the end from the inside of the yarn ball and alternately knit with the strand from the inside and the strand from the outside.

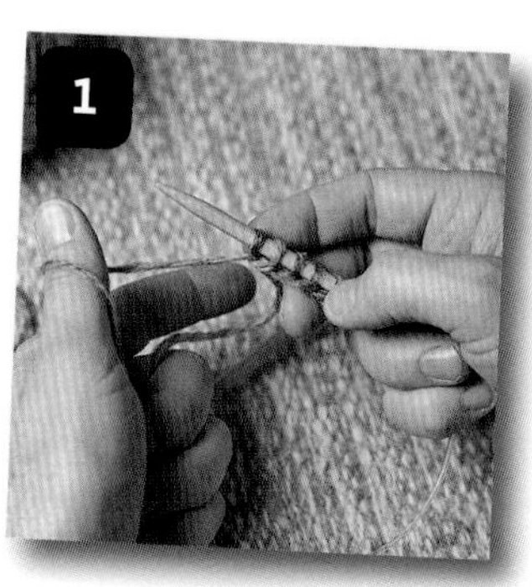

Photo 2: Before you start knitting in the round, make sure that the cast-on row is not twisted.

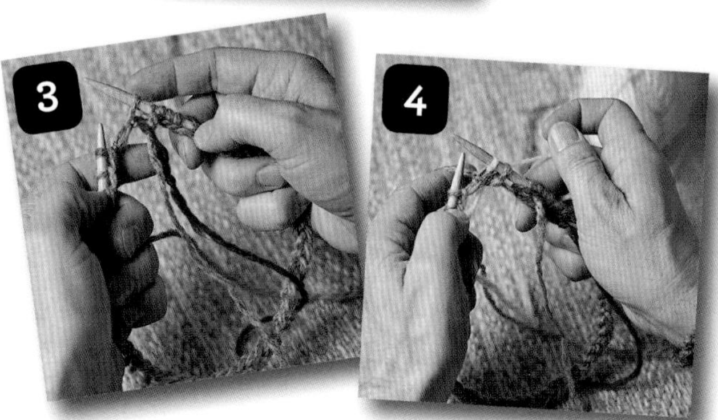

Photos 3, 4, and 5: Alternate yarns on each stitch.

MATERIALS

YARN: Rauma Vamsegarn (CYCA #4, worsted/afghan/aran; 100% wool; 91 yd/83 m / 50 g)

NEEDLES: 16 in / 40 cm circular and set of 5 dpn, U.S. size 8-10 / 5-6 mm

RECOMMENDED GAUGE: 14-16 sts = 4 in / 10 cm

Make a gauge swatch to determine whether to go up or down on needle size. We knitted our slippers with U.S. size 10 / 6 mm with a gauge of 16 sts in 4 in / 10 cm before felting.

With one strand of yarn and short circular or dpn, CO 56 (60, 64) sts (we recommend a 16 in / 40 cm circular). Using two strands of yarn and alternating them on every stitch, knit 3 rnds.

HEEL

Work back and forth in stockinette st. You can work the heel with a circular—place the instep sts on a holder while you work the heel sts.

WORKING BACK AND FORTH WITH 2 STRANDS

NOTE: When knitting or purling into a stitch worked previously with 2 strands, work as one stitch.

Row 1: K14 (15, 16), knitting last st with both strands; turn.
Row 2: Sl 1, p27 (29, 31), purling last st with both strands; turn.
Row 3: Sl 1, k27 (29, 31), knitting last st with both strands; turn.
Row 4: Sl 1, p27 (29, 31), purling last st with both strands; turn.
Row 5: Sl 1, k27 (29, 31), knitting last st with both strands; turn.
Row 6: Sl 1, p27 (29, 31), purling last st with both strands; turn.
Row 7: Sl 1, k27 (29, 31), knitting last st with both strands; turn.
Row 8: Sl 1, p27 (29, 31), purling last st with both strands; turn.
Row 9: Sl 1, k27 (29, 31), knitting last st with both strands; turn.
Row 10: Sl 1, p27 (29, 31), purling last st with both strands; turn.
Row 11: Sl 1, k27 (29, 31), knitting last st with both strands; turn.
Row 12: Sl 1, p27 (29, 31), purling last st with both strands; turn.
Row 13: Sl 1, k27 (29, 31), knitting last st with both strands; turn.

HEEL TURN

Continue slipping the first st of every row.
Row 14: P13 (15, 17), p2tog, p1 with both strands; turn.
Row 15: K3 (5, 7), k2tog, k1 with both strands; turn.
Row 16: P4 (6, 8), p2tog, p1 with both strands; turn.
Row 17: K5 (7, 9), k2tog, k1 with both strands; turn.
Row 18: P6 (8, 10), p2tog, p1 with both strands; turn.
Row 19: K7 (9, 11), k2tog, k1 with both strands; turn.
Row 20: P8 (10, 12), p2tog, p1 with both strands; turn.
Row 21: K9 (11, 13), k2tog, k1 with both strands; turn.
Row 22: P10 (12, 14), p2tog, p1 with both strands; turn.
Row 23: K11 (13, 15), k2tog, k1 with both strands; turn.
Row 24: P12 (14, 16), p2tog, p1 with both strands; turn.
Row 25: K13 (15, 17), k2tog with both strands; turn.
(**NOTE:** This row ends with k2tog and not k1 as previously.)
Row 26: P13 (15, 17), p2tog, p1 with both strands; turn.

Purling when changing strands on each stitch. The strand you are not using (here, the gray strand) is closer to you.

Purl with the other strand (white).

The strands trade places—the white is now closer to you.

NOTE: Don't forget to alternate the two strands on every stitch. When we are picking up and knitting stitches along the edge of the heel flap, we insert the needle under one loop of the edge stitch.
When working the heel back and forth as here, the result is an odd number of sts along the edge. Make sure you pick up the same number of sts on each side of the heel flap.

Rnd 1: Ssk, k6 (7, 8). Place a marker for beginning of rnd at the center of the sole, k7 (8, 9), pick up and knit 7 sts evenly spaced along the edge sts of heel flap, k28 (30, 32) sts from holder, pick up and knit 7 sts evenly spaced along other side of heel flap and end with k7 (8, 9) sts on sole = 56 (60, 64) sts total.
Rnds 2-34 (2-37, 2-40): Knit around.

TOE SHAPING

Rnd 35 (38, 41): *K1, k2tog, k8 (9, 10), k2tog, k1*; rep from * to * around.
Rnd 36 (39, 42): K48 (52, 56).
Rnd 37 (40, 43): *K1, k2tog, k6 (7, 8), k2tog, k1*; rep from * to * around.
Rnd 38 (41, 44): K40 (44, 48).
Rnd 39 (42, 45): *K1, k2tog, k4 (5, 6), k2tog, k1*; rep from * to * around.
Rnd 40 (43, 46): K32, (36, 40).
Rnd 41 (44, 47): *K1, k2tog, k2 (3, 4), k2tog, k1*; rep from * to * around.
Rnd 42 (45, 48): K24 (28, 32).
Rnd 43 (last rnd size S): K1, k2tog, k2tog, k1*; rep from * to * around.
Rnd 46 (49) (last rnd size M): *K1, k2tog, k1 (2), k2tog, k1*; rep from * to * around.
Rnd 50: K24.
Rnd 51 (last rnd size L): Work (k1, k2tog, k2tog, k1) around.
Cut yarn and draw both strands through the rem 16 sts. Pull tight to gather sts around hole at tip of toe. Weave in all ends neatly on WS.
Gently steam press slippers before felting.
Felt slippers on delicate cycle, 104°F / 40°C, for 120 minutes. The felting is always best when we can see that the slippers look quite small.

Purl with the gray yarn.

Picking up stitches along heel flap. When you slip the first stitch of every row on the heel flap, you will create a chain edge which you can then easily pick up and knit into.

Pick up and knit sts in the chain edge.

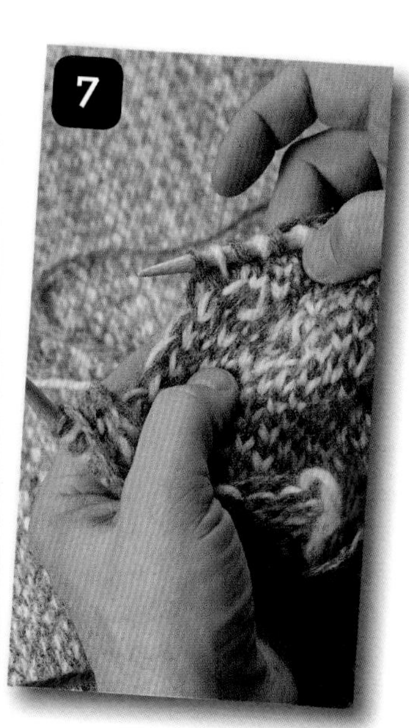

Alternate the two strands throughout.

THREE STYLES OF SLIPPERS

SLIPPERS WITH A LONG CUFF

For these basic slippers, work 18 rnds for the cuff before beginning the heel flap. If you make your first pair with two contrasting colors, it will be easier to adjust the number of rounds in the foot if you need a longer or shorter slipper.

SLIPPERS WITH A SHORT CUFF

Some of our slippers have a shorter cuff. A short cuff can be worked back and forth in stockinette stitch in a pattern or you can knit it back and forth and decorate it after felting. Some of these shorter cuffs have a split at center front and stand up.

CLOG SLIPPERS

For the clog-style slippers, knit 3 rounds before working the heel flap.

PATTERN KNITTING

With two-color stranded knitting, the strands are twisted around each other on the wrong side whenever there is a long stretch between colors in the pattern. We knit 3 or 4 stitches and then twist the strands. That way, the knitting is more even and the pattern strands won't pull in as much as when there are long, unsecured floats. At the same time, don't pull too hard when you twist the strands—occasionally check the wrong side to make sure that the floats lie smoothly on the surface. If you pull the strands too hard, the piece will shrink more than it should. If there are long floats in the pattern, the slippers will look better once they've been steam pressed.

Photo 1: Begin at the base of the stitch you want to cover.

Photo 2: Follow the path of the stitch and sew under the base of the stitch above the one you are covering.

EMBROIDERED DUPLICATE STITCH

Sometimes it is easier to embroider on a pattern or a motif than to knit it in. When you are using only a small amount of a color in a pattern or motif, it is easier to embroider it on. If an entire motif is to be embroidered in, mark one stitch in the knitting to correspond to one stitch in the motif as a guide. Embroidered motifs will look nicer after felting than motifs that are knitted in. Before embroidering, steam press the fabric to make it easier to embroider. We also steam press after the embroidery is complete.

Photo 3: Make sure that the embroidery thread lies smoothly over the stitch.

Photo 4: Sew through the starting point at the base of the stitch and bring the needle up at the base of the next stitch to be covered.

Photo 5: Work stitch after stitch the same way.

Photo 6: Do not pull too hard on the threads.

Photo 7: and so forth!

Some stitch charts are upside down, and you'll see why when you embroider, for example, the slippers with Christmas trees and packages. The stitches are upside down when you put on the slippers. On, for example, Magnus, you can count stitches from the edge of the cuff, and it seemed natural to us that the stitches point downwards when we embroider.

Chapter 4

Life at the cabin

Slippers for lazy days with your family and friends at the cabin. Knit lots of slippers so everyone visiting can have a pair.

STRIKKEOPPSKRIFTER
89
STRIKKEOPPSKRIFTER
HUSFLIDEN's

Slippers with a diamond panel

These slippers have a classic diamond pattern and long cuffs. The "circle" motif is one of the most used panels in Norwegian knitting, either alone, as on these slippers, or combined with a cross for *kross og kringle* on Setesdal sweaters. The pattern is so easy to work that it almost knits itself in stranded two-color knitting.

MATERIALS

YARN: Rauma Vamsegarn (CYCA #4, worsted/afghan/aran; 100% wool; 91 yd/83 m / 50 g)
2-3 balls Bright Pink V56
1 ball Off-White V01
1 ball Light Lilac V71

NEEDLES: U.S. size 8-10 / 5-6 mm: circular and set of 5 dpn

RECOMMENDED GAUGE: 14-16 sts = 4 in / 10 cm

NOTES

All sizes begin with the same stitch count so the cuff will be large enough for you to get the slippers on your feet after felting.
For additional details about knitting the slippers, refer to Chapter 3, Basic Slippers, pages 15-19.

With one strand of Light Lilac V71, CO 64 sts for all sizes; join, being careful not to twist cast-on row. The bottom row of squares on the chart is the cast-on row. Follow the charted pattern until 1 rnd remains. Don't forget to twist the yarns around each other regularly to avoid long floats. Work the single color rounds with two strands of the same color, changing strands with each stitch.
On the last rnd of the chart, decrease evenly spaced around:
SIZE S: decrease 8 sts = 56 sts rem.
SIZE M: decrease 4 sts = 60 sts rem.
SIZE L: decrease 0 sts = 64 sts rem.
Continue with Bright Pink V56 only.

HEEL

ROW 1: K14 (15, 16), knitting last st with both strands; turn.
ROW 2: Sl 1, p27 (29, 31), purling last st with both strands; turn.
Work another 11 rows back and forth in stockinette over the 28 (30, 32) heel sts, always slipping the first st.

HEEL TURN

ROW 14: P13 (15, 17), p2tog, p1 with both strands; turn.
ROW 15: K3 (5, 7), k2tog, k1 with both strands; turn.
ROWS 16-23: Continue in stockinette and shaping, with 1 more st before the decrease on each row (the decrease joins the sts before/after the gap).
ROW 24: P12 (14, 16), p2tog, p1 with both strands; turn.
ROW 25: K13 (15, 17), k2tog with both strands; turn. (**NOTE:** This row ends with k2tog and not k1 as previously.)
ROW 26: P13 (15, 17), p2tog, p1 with both strands; turn.

FOOT

SET-UP RND: Ssk, k6 (7, 8). Pm at center of sole, k7 (8, 9), pick up and knit 7 sts evenly spaced across one side of the heel flap, k28 (30, 32) across instep, pick up and knit 7 sts evenly spaced across other side of heel flap and k7 (8, 9) on sole. The beginning of the rnd is at center of sole.
FOOT: Knit 33 (36, 39) rnds on the 56 (60, 64) sts of foot. Divide the sts onto 4 dpn with 14 (15, 16) sts on each needle. Shape toe as follows, with 8 sts decreased on each decrease rnd.
RND 1 (DECREASE RND): At beginning of each needle: K1, k2tog. At end of each needle: K2tog, k1.
RND 2: Knit.
Repeat Rnds 1-2 until 16 (20, 16) sts rem. Cut yarn and draw end through remaining sts. Pull tight and weave in all ends neatly on WS. Steam press and then felt slippers.

Chart for Diamond

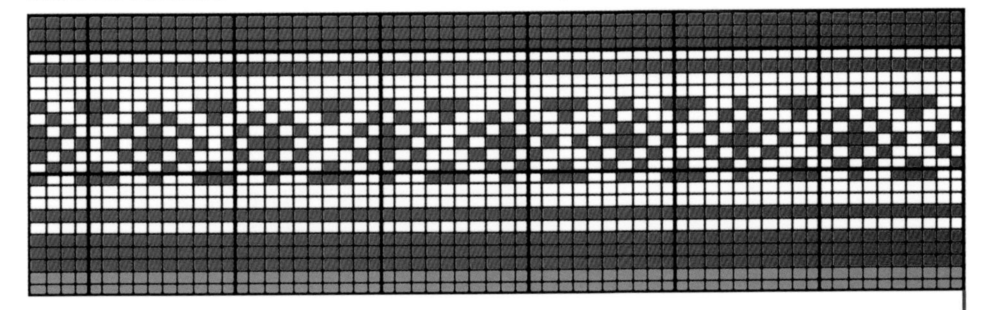

Center back—Begin here

Slippers with eight-petaled roses

These slippers are great for cold winter days when you don't need to go outside and can stay cozy inside. Light some candles, turn on some music, and curl up in a comfy chair with your knitting and a delicious drink. The idea for this pattern came from a project using leftover yarns, begun early in the 1990s but never finished.

MATERIALS

Yarn: Rauma Vamsegarn (CYCA #4, worsted/afghan/ aran; 100% wool; 91 yd/83 m / 50 g)
3 balls Black V36
1 ball Red V18
1 ball Light Lilac V71
1 ball Yellow V25
1 ball Bright Royal Blue V37

Needles: U.S. size 8-10 / 5-6 mm: circular and set of 5 dpn

Recommended Gauge: 14-16 sts = 4 in / 10 cm

NOTES

All sizes begin with the same stitch count so the cuff will be large enough for you to get the slippers on your feet after felting.

If there are more than 4 sts between color changes, twist the yarns around each other to avoid long floats.

For additional details about knitting the slippers, refer to Chapter 3, Basic Slippers, pages 15-19.

With Black V36 and circular, CO 75 sts; join, being careful not to twist cast-on row. Work following the chart—the first row of the chart = cast-on row.

On the last rnd of the charted pattern, decrease evenly spaced around as follows:

Size S: decrease 19 sts = 56 sts rem.
Size M: decrease 15 sts = 60 sts rem.
Size L: decrease 11 sts = 64 sts rem.

Continue to the heel and heel shaping with Black V36, alternating the two strands on every stitch.

Chart for Eight-Petaled Roses

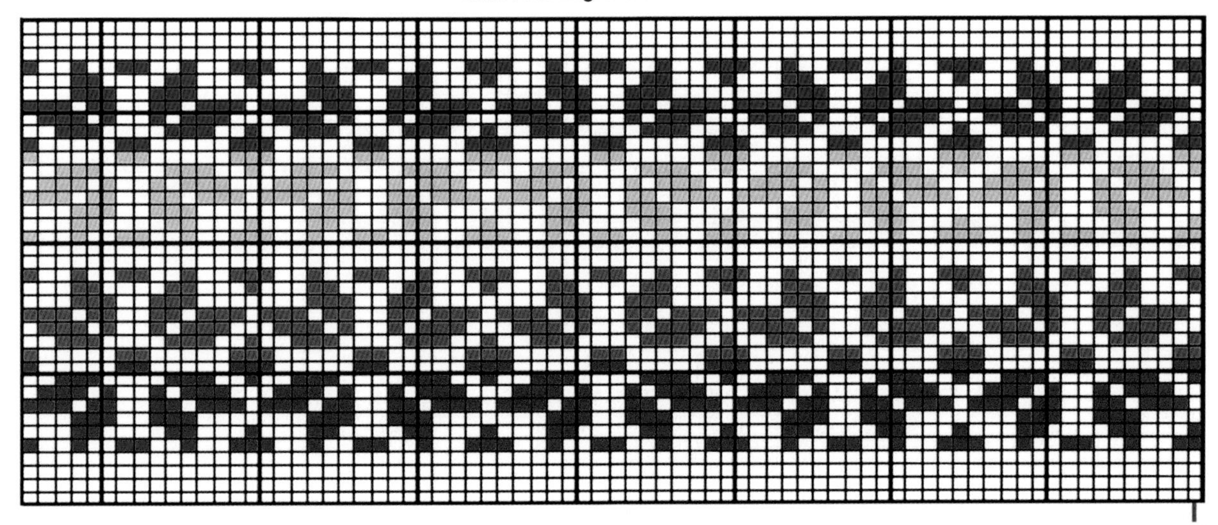

HEEL

Row 1: K14 (15, 16), knitting last st with both strands; turn.

Row 2: Sl 1, p27 (29, 31), purling last st with both strands; turn.

Work another 11 rows back and forth in stockinette over the 28 (30, 32) heel sts, always slipping the first st.

HEEL TURN

Row 14: P13 (15, 17), p2tog, p1 with both strands; turn.
Row 15: K3 (5, 7), k2tog, k1 with both strands; turn.
Rows 16-23: Continue in stockinette and shaping, with 1 more st before the decrease on each row (the decrease joins the sts before/after the gap).
Row 24: P12 (14, 16), p2tog, p1 with both strands; turn.
Row 25: K13 (15, 17), k2tog with both strands; turn. (**NOTE:** This row ends with k2tog and not k1 as previously.)
Row 26: P13 (15, 17), p2tog, p1 with both strands; turn.

FOOT

Set-up Rnd: Ssk, k6 (7, 8). Pm at center of sole, k7 (8, 9), pick up and knit 7 sts evenly spaced across one side of the heel flap, k28 (30, 32) across instep, pick up and knit 7 sts evenly spaced across other side of heel flap and k7 (8, 9) on sole. The beginning of the rnd is at center of sole.
Foot: Following the chart, beginning at the stitch and rnd for your size, knit 33 (36, 39) rnds on the 56 (60, 64) sts of foot.
Divide the sts onto 4 dpn with 14 (15, 16) sts on each needle. Working with 2 strands of Black only, shape toe as follows, with 8 sts decreased on each decrease rnd.
Rnd 1 (decrease rnd): At beginning of each needle: K1, k2tog. At end of each needle: K2tog, k1.
Rnd 2: Knit.
Repeat Rnds 1-2 until 16 (20, 16) sts rem. Cut yarn and draw end through remaining sts. Pull tight and weave in all ends neatly on WS.
Steam press and then felt slippers.

Chart for Foot—Eight-Petaled Roses

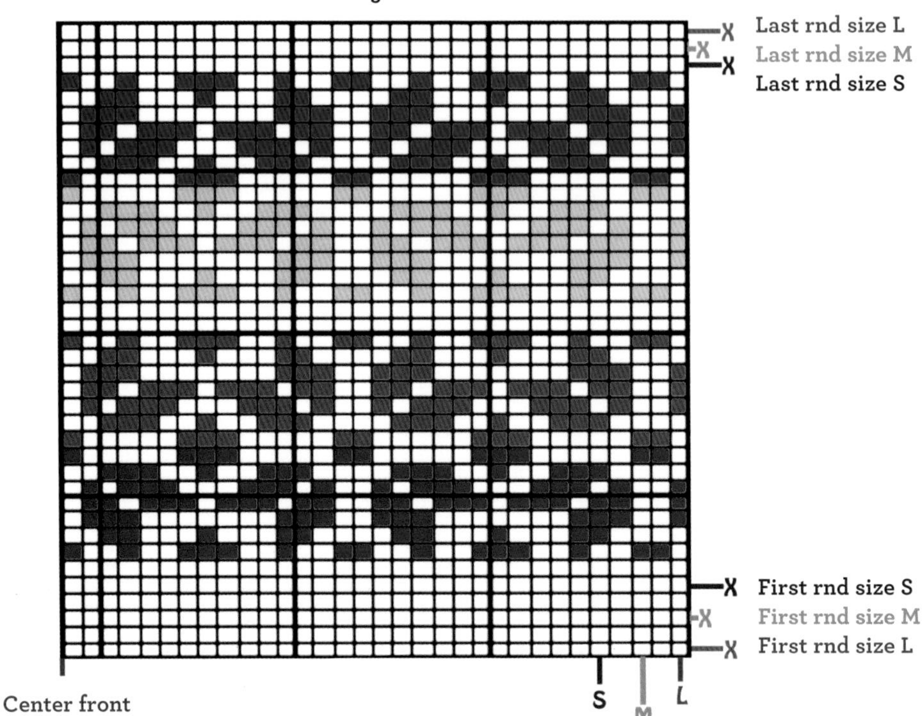

Three-color clog slippers

These are slippers for Dad, knitted in black and gray for a men's design. The graphic pattern could be considered quite traditional, but it came more or less of its own accord. The red stripe defines the slippers' form quite well. The slippers show how effective the cast-on with one strand can be—the edge rolls for a nice line after felting.

MATERIALS

Yarn: Rauma Vamsegarn (CYCA #4, worsted/afghan/aran; 100% wool; 91 yd/83 m / 50 g)
2 balls Ebony V10
2 balls Gray Heather V13
1 ball Dark Red V23

Needles: U.S. size 8-10 / 5-6 mm: circular and set of 5 dpn

Recommended Gauge: 14-16 sts = 4 in / 10 cm

NOTE

For additional details about knitting the slippers, refer to Chapter 3, Basic Slippers, pages 15-19.

With one strand of Dark Red and circular, CO 56 (60, 64) sts; join, being careful not to twist cast-on row. Join second strand of Red and knit 1 rnd, alternating the 2 strands of yarn on each stitch. Cut Dark Red and change to Ebony. Knit 2 rnds, alternating two strands of yarn on every stitch.
Now work the heel in charted pattern and as follows:

HEEL

Row 1: K14 (15, 16), knitting last st with both strands; turn.
Row 2: Sl 1, p27 (29, 31), purling last st with both strands; turn.
Work another 11 rows back and forth in stockinette over the 28 (30, 32) heel sts, always slipping the first st.

Chart for Heel

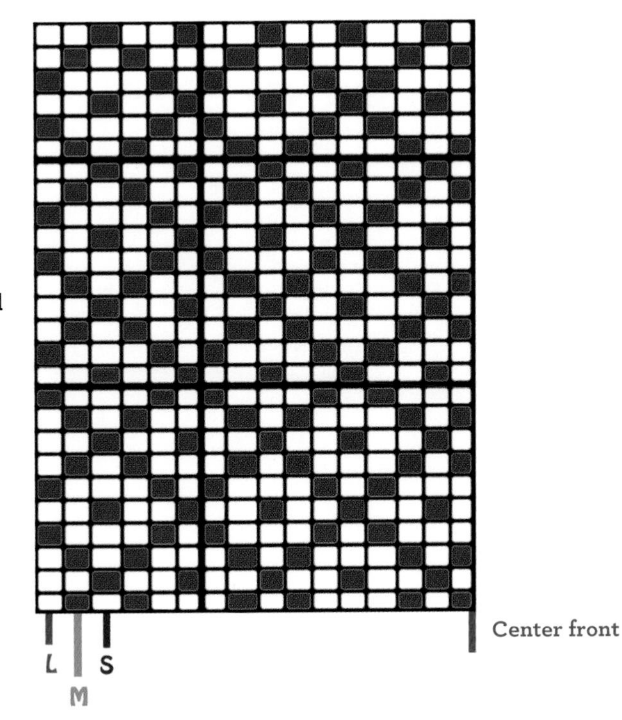

HEEL TURN

Row 14: P13 (15, 17), p2tog, p1 with both strands; turn.
Row 15: K3 (5, 7), k2tog, k1 with both strands; turn.
Rows 16-23: Continue stockinette and shaping, with 1 more st before the decrease on each row (the decrease joins the sts before/after the gap).
Row 24: P12 (14, 16), p2tog, p1 with both strands; turn.
Row 25: K13 (15, 17), k2tog with both strands; turn. (**NOTE:** This row ends with k2tog and not k1 as previously.)
Row 26: P13 (15, 17), p2tog, p1 with both strands; turn.

FOOT

Set-up Rnd: Ssk, k6 (7, 8). Pm at center of sole, k7 (8, 9), pick up and knit 7 sts evenly spaced across one side of the heel flap, k28 (30, 32) across instep, pick up and knit 7 sts evenly spaced across other side of heel flap and k7 (8, 9) on sole. The beginning of the rnd is at center of sole.
Foot: Following the chart, beginning at the stitch and rnd for your size, knit 33 (36, 39) rnds on the 56 (60, 64) sts of foot.
Divide the sts onto 4 dpn with 14 (15, 16) sts on each needle. With Ebony only, shape toe as follows, with 8 sts decreased on each decrease rnd.
Rnd 1 (decrease rnd): At beginning of each needle: K1, k2tog. At end of each needle: K2tog, k1.
Rnd 2: Knit.
Repeat Rnds 1-2 until 16 (20, 16) sts rem. Cut yarn and draw end through remaining sts. Pull tight and weave in all ends neatly on WS. Steam press and then felt slippers.

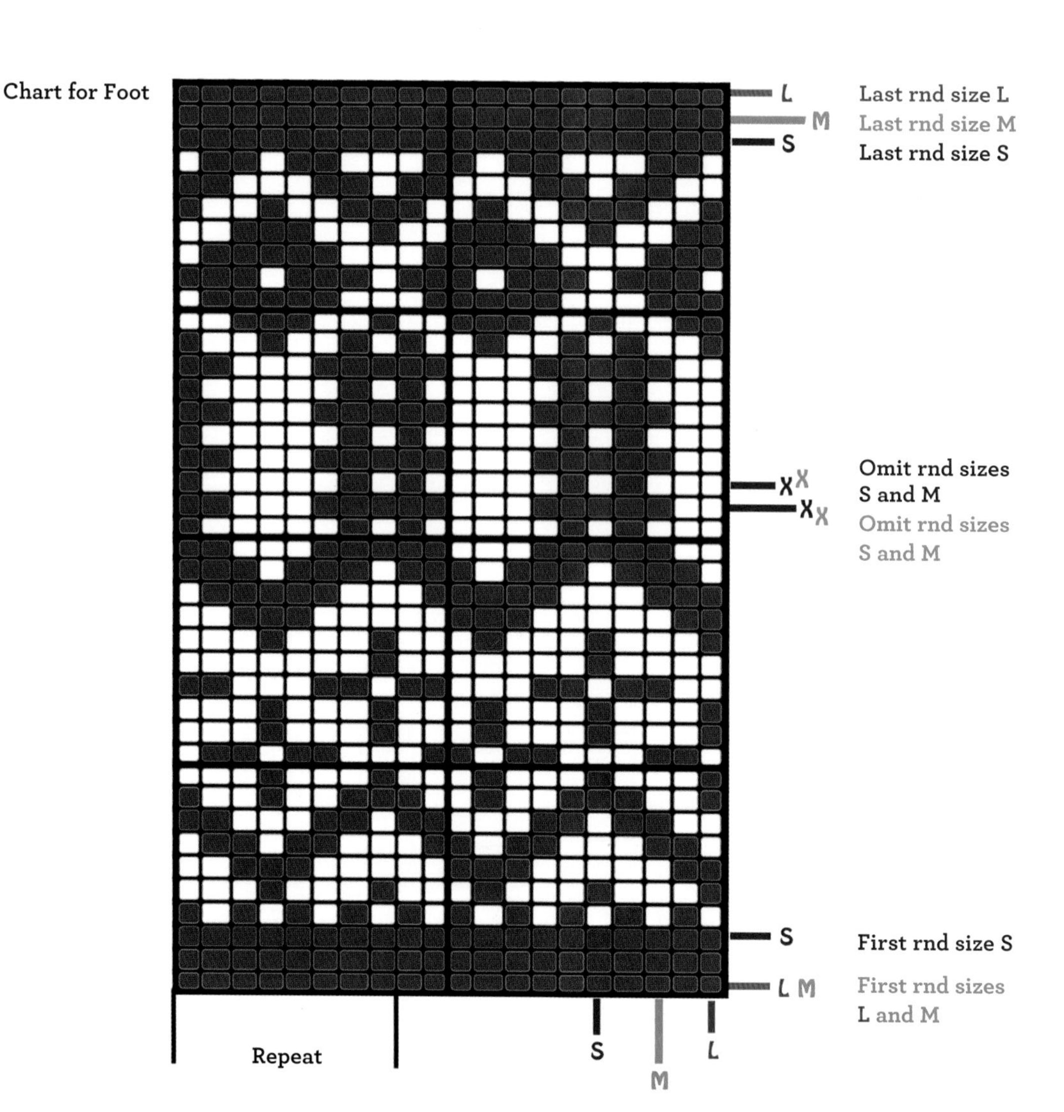

Slippers with a pattern on the sole

These slippers have different patterns on the instep and sole and you'll need to twist the yarns frequently on the instep to avoid long floats. We knitted this pair in the Medium size. The pattern knitting was a little tighter than with a single color of yarn or embroidery, but the shaping came out well. If you wear the slippers immediately after felting, you can shape them for a right and left foot.

MATERIALS

YARN: Rauma Vamsegarn (CYCA #4, worsted/afghan/aran; 100% wool; 91 yd/83 m / 50 g)
2 balls Evergreen V88
2 balls Gray Heather V13

NEEDLES: U.S. size 8-10 / 5-6 mm: circular and set of 5 dpn

RECOMMENDED GAUGE: 14-16 sts = 4 in / 10 cm

NOTES

If there are more than 4 sts between color changes, twist the yarns around each other to avoid long floats.
For additional details about knitting the slippers, refer to Chapter 3, Basic Slippers, pages 15-19.

With one strand of Evergreen and circular, CO 56 (60, 64) sts; join, being careful not to twist cast-on row. Join second strand of Evergreen and knit 3 rnds, alternating two strands of yarn on each stitch. Attach Gray Heather and begin Heel in charted pattern as follows:

HEEL

ROW 1: K14 (15, 16), knitting last st with both strands; turn.
ROW 2: Sl 1, p27 (29, 31), purling last st with both strands; turn.
Work another 11 rows back and forth in stockinette over the 28 (30, 32) heel sts, always slipping the first st.

HEEL TURN

ROW 14: P13 (15, 17), p2tog, p1 with both strands; turn.
ROW 15: K3 (5, 7), k2tog, k1 with both strands; turn.
ROWS 16-23: Continue in stockinette and shaping, with 1 more st before the decrease on each row (the decrease joins the sts before/after the gap).
ROW 24: P12 (14, 16), p2tog, p1 with both strands; turn.
ROW 25: K13 (15, 17), k2tog with both strands; turn.
(**NOTE:** This row ends with k2tog and not k1 as previously.)
ROW 26: P13 (15, 17), p2tog, p1 with both strands; turn.

FOOT

Following the chart for your size, work the foot:
SET-UP RND: Ssk, k6 (7, 8). Pm at center of sole, k7 (8, 9), pick up and knit 7 sts evenly spaced across one side of the heel flap, k28 (30, 32) across instep, pick up and knit 7 sts evenly spaced across other side of heel flap and k7 (8, 9) on sole. The beginning of the rnd is at center of sole.
FOOT: Knit 33 (36, 39) rnds on the 56 (60, 64) sts of foot. Divide the sts onto 4 dpn with 14 (15, 16) sts on each needle. With Evergreen only, shape toe as follows, with 8 sts decreased on each decrease rnd.
RND 1 (DECREASE RND): At beginning of each needle: K1, k2tog. At end of each needle: K2tog, k1.
RND 2: Knit.
Repeat Rnds 1-2 until 16 (20, 16) sts rem. Cut yarn and draw end through remaining sts. Pull tight and weave in all ends neatly on WS. Steam press and then felt slippers.

Chart for Heel

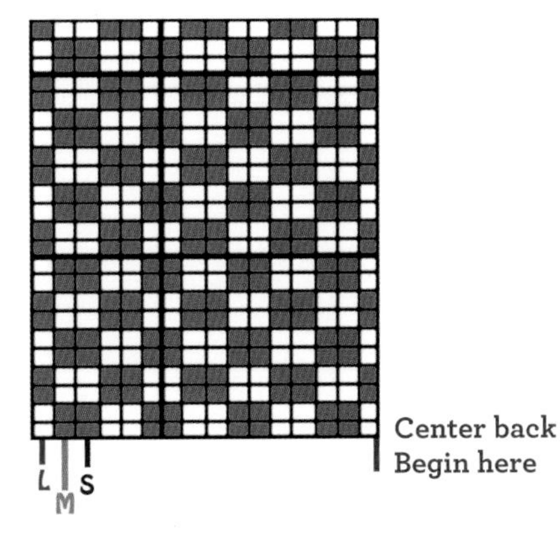

Chart for Sole and Instep, Size S

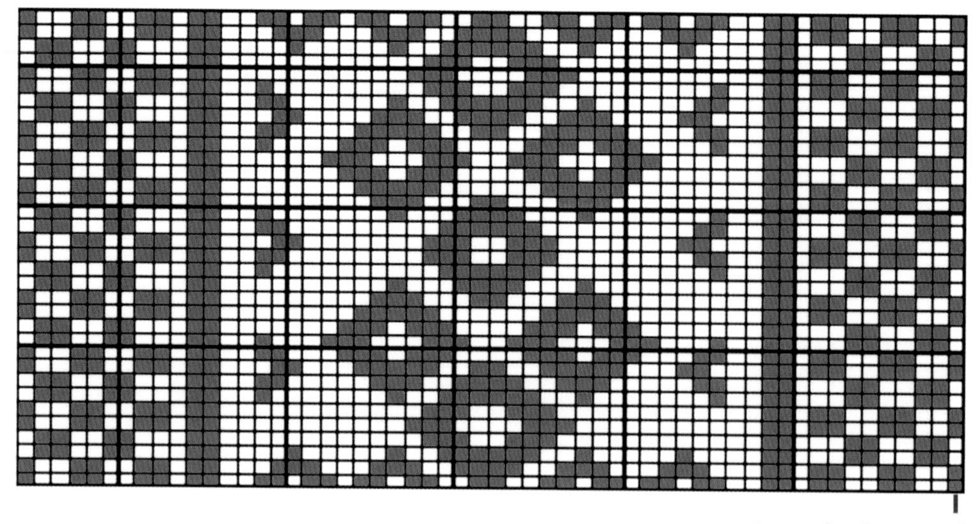

Chart for Sole and Instep, Size M

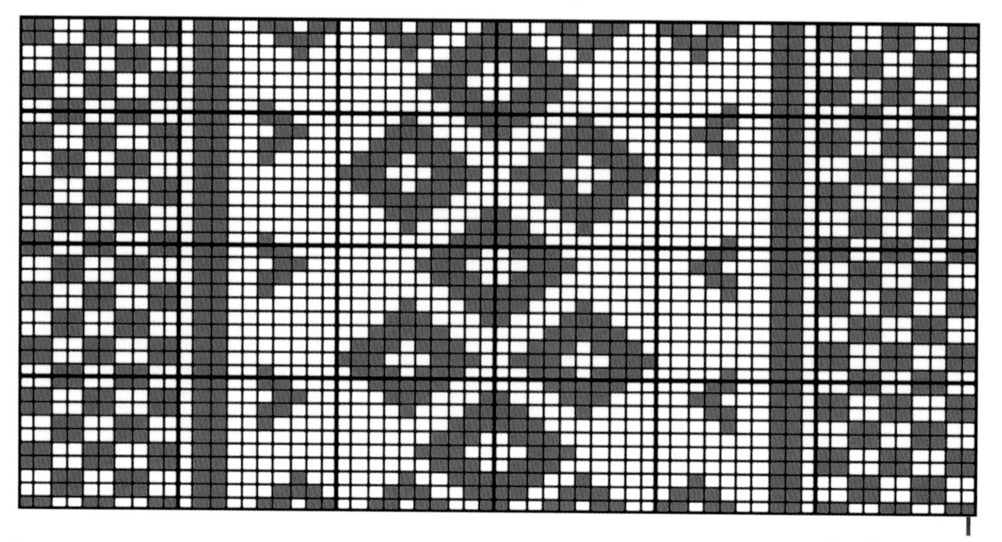

Chart for Sole and Instep, Size L

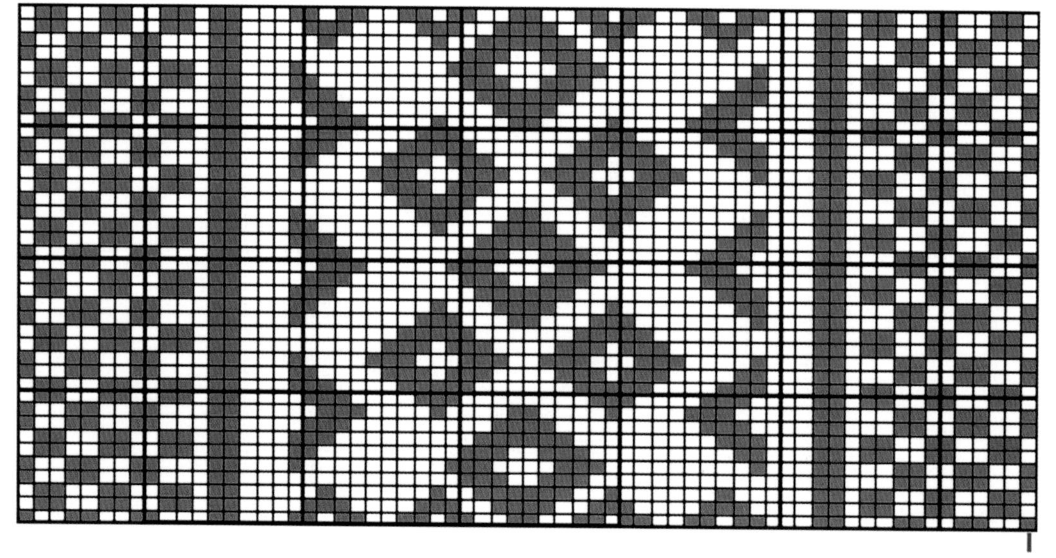

Slippers with two-color block patterns on the sole and heel. Twist the two strands around each other every 3-4 stitches on single-color sections in the pattern bands.

Slippers with decorative bands and clasps

These slippers were inspired by all of the old knitted jackets found in cabins everywhere in Norway—those that aren't considered fine enough for everyday wear, those that "hang out" in the cabin. These jackets are often decorated with woven bands and pewter clasps.

MATERIALS

Yarn: Rauma Vamsegarn (CYCA #4, worsted/afghan/aran; 100% wool; 91 yd/83 m / 50 g)
2-3 balls Cranberry Red V35

Notions: 53¼ in / 135 cm decorative band
4 clasp sets
sewing thread and needle

Needles: U.S. size 8-10 / 5-6 mm: circular and set of 5 dpn

Recommended Gauge: 14-16 sts = 4 in / 10 cm

NOTE

For additional details about knitting the slippers, refer to Chapter 3, Basic Slippers, pages 15-19.

With one strand of yarn and circular, CO 56 (60, 64) sts. Add second strand and work back and forth in stockinette, alternating the two strands on every stitch. Always slip the first st of the row when working back and forth
Rows 1 and 3: Sl 1, purl to end of row = 56 (60, 64) sts.
Row 2: Sl 1, knit to end of row = 56 (60, 64) sts.

HEEL

Always slip the first st of the row when working back and forth.
Row 1: K42 (45, 48), knitting last st with both strands; turn.
Row 2: Sl 1, p27 (29, 31), purling last st with both strands; turn.
Work another 11 rows back and forth in stockinette over the 28 (30, 32) heel sts, always slipping the first st.

HEEL TURN

Row 14: P13 (15, 17), p2tog, p1 with both strands; turn.
Row 15: K3 (5, 7), k2tog, k1 with both strands; turn.
Rows 16-23: Continue in stockinette and shaping, with 1 more st before the decrease on each row (the decrease joins the sts before/after the gap).
Row 24: P12 (14, 16), p2tog, p1 with both strands; turn.
Row 25: K13 (15, 17), k2tog with both strands; turn. (**NOTE:** This row ends with k2tog and not k1 as previously.)
Row 26: P13 (15, 17), p2tog, p1 with both strands; turn.

FOOT

Set-up Row 1: Ssk, k6 (7, 8). Pm at center of sole, k7 (8, 9), pick up and knit 7 sts evenly spaced across one side of the heel flap; knit to end of row.
Set-up Row 2: Purl until 7 (8, 9) sts past marker at center of sole, pick up and purl 7 sts evenly spaced across side of heel flap; purl to end of row.
Foot: Work 13 (15, 17) rows back and forth in stockinette.
Rnd 14 (16, 18): Join and knit in the round.
Continue around in stockinette until there are a total of 33 (36, 39) rows/rnds from beginning of foot.
Divide the sts onto 4 dpn with 14 (15, 16) sts on each needle. Shape toe as follows, with 8 sts decreased on each decrease rnd.
Rnd 1 (decrease rnd): At beginning of each needle: K1, k2tog. At end of each needle: K2tog, k1.
Rnd 2: Knit.
Repeat Rnds 1-2 until 16 (20, 16) sts rem. Cut yarn and draw end through remaining sts. Pull tight and weave in all ends neatly on WS.

FINISHING

Steam press and then felt slippers. After slippers have completely dried, sew on decorative bands and clasps.

Décor
COTON PERLÉ BRILLANTÉ CB « A LA

Royal slippers with coat-of-arms

Royal slippers with lions in commemoration of Norway's Constitution Day in 1814. These are naturally suitable as bathroom slippers, where most people can sit on the "throne," be independent, enjoy the quiet, and read a little in the old weekly magazines.

Bathroom slippers: an idea from Japan

We were at a traditional restaurant in Kyoto, where customers were required to remove their shoes outside the main entrance. The shoes were placed in a cupboard and house slippers were available for everyone to wear in the restaurant, which had traditional tatami mats on the floor. I had to go to the restroom and, when I got to the bathroom, I found a pair of orange slippers outside the door. I was told to use these slippers in the restroom. I took off my restaurant slippers and put on the orange slippers and went into the men's room. When I was back at my table, I noticed that I still had the orange slippers on and the word "toilet" was written on them. I had forgotten to change back to the restaurant slippers! That was an embarrassing moment but everyone was so polite that it ended up okay—and I had a good story to tell.

CARLOS' RESTROOM EXPERIENCE IN JAPAN

MATERIALS

YARN: Rauma Vamsegarn (CYCA #4, worsted/afghan/aran; 100% wool; 91 yd/83 m / 50 g)
3-4 balls Blue V82
1 ball Red V18
1 ball Gold V46
1 ball Off-White V01

NEEDLES: U.S. size 8-10 / 5-6 mm: circular and set of 5 dpn

RECOMMENDED GAUGE: 14-16 sts = 4 in / 10 cm

NOTE

For additional details about knitting the slippers, refer to Chapter 3, Basic Slippers, pages 15-19.

With one strand of Blue and circular, CO 56 (60, 64) sts. Attach second strand of Blue and alternate strands on every stitch (work with 2 strands throughout). Always slip the first st of the row when working back and forth. Knit 10 rows in garter st and then join the short cuff: K28 (30, 32) to center back, pm, k28 (30, 32). The rnd begins at center back marker. Knit 3 rnds.

HEEL

Continue with 2 strands of Blue. Always slip the first st of the row when working back and forth.
ROW 1: K14 (15, 16), knitting last st with both strands; turn.
ROW 2: Sl 1, p27 (29, 31), purling last st with both strands; turn.
Work another 11 rows back and forth in stockinette over the 28 (30, 32) heel sts, always slipping the first st.

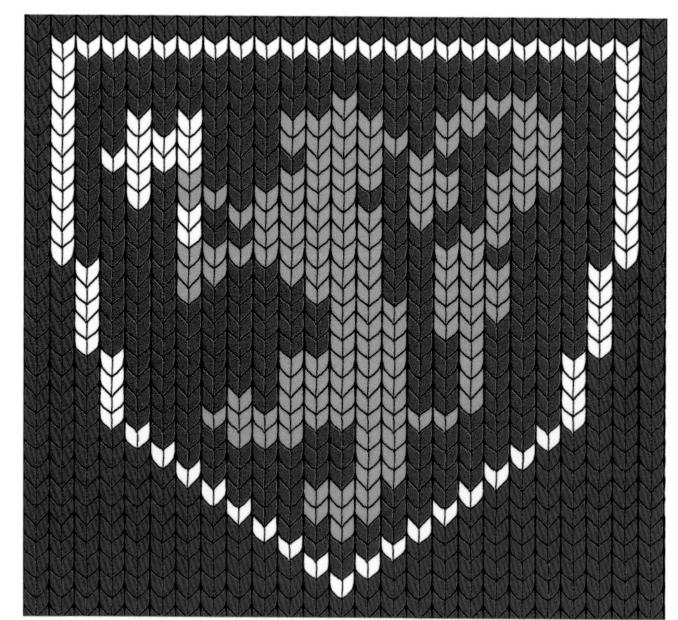

**Embroidery Chart
Slipper 1**

HEEL TURN

Row 14: P13 (15, 17), p2tog, p1 with both strands; turn.
Row 15: K3 (5, 7), k2tog, k1 with both strands; turn.
Rows 16-23: Continue in stockinette and shaping, with 1 more st before the decrease on each row (the decrease joins the sts before/after the gap).
Row 24: P12 (14, 16), p2tog, p1 with both strands; turn.
Row 25: K13 (15, 17), k2tog with both strands; turn. (**NOTE:** This row ends with k2tog and not k1 as previously.)
Row 26: P13 (15, 17), p2tog, p1 with both strands; turn.

FOOT

Set-up Rnd: Ssk, k6 (7, 8). Pm at center of sole, k7 (8, 9), pick up and knit 7 sts evenly spaced across one side of the heel flap, k28 (30, 32) across instep, pick up and knit 7 sts evenly spaced across other side of heel flap and k7 (8, 9) on sole. The beginning of the rnd is at center of sole.
Foot: Knit 33 (36, 39) rnds on the 56 (60, 64) sts of foot. Divide the sts onto 4 dpn with 14 (15, 16) sts on each needle. Shape toe as follows, with 8 sts decreased on each decrease rnd.
Rnd 1 (decrease rnd): At beginning of each needle: K1, k2tog. At end of each needle: K2tog, k1.
Rnd 2: Knit.
Repeat Rnds 1-2 until 16 (20, 16) sts rem. Cut yarn and draw end through remaining sts. Pull tight and weave in all ends neatly on WS.

FINISHING

Steam press slippers. Embroider the charted motif using duplicate stitch and Off-White, Gold, and Red yarn. Steam press the embroidery and then felt the slippers.

**Embroidery Chart
Slipper 2**

Læstadius Preaches to the Sami (1840), painted by Francois-Auguste Biard (1799-1882); Northern Norway's Art Museum, Tromsø.

Chapter 5

Sami moccasins

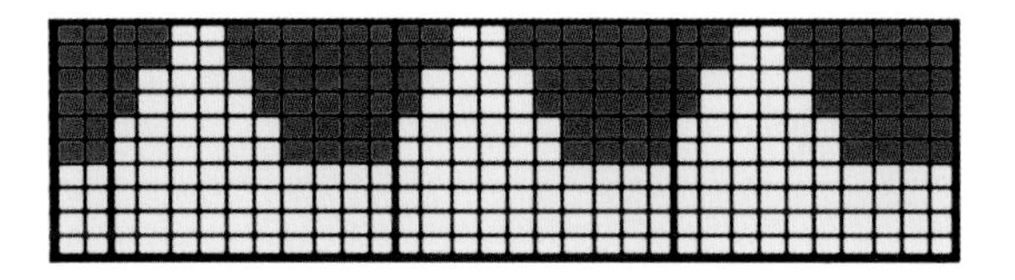

There are so many interesting and fascinating types of footwear to draw inspiration from! For the next five pairs of slippers, we took our ideas from the Sami moccasins called "skaller." *Skaller* are traditional Sami winter footwear, sewn with reindeer skin with the hair side out and decorated with woven bands and tassels.

Kautokeino slippers

The pattern for these slippers was inspired by a woven *skalle* band from 1944, for men from Kautokeino. The long cuffs of the slippers make them cozy and very warm.

Chart

MATERIALS

YARN: Rauma Vamsegarn (CYCA #4, worsted/afghan/aran; 100% wool; 91 yd/83 m / 50 g)
3 balls Blue V82
1 ball Bright Red V24
1 ball White V00

NEEDLES: U.S. size 8-10 / 5-6 mm: circular and set of 5 dpn

RECOMMENDED GAUGE: 14-16 sts = 4 in / 10 cm

NOTES

All sizes begin with the same stitch count so the cuff will be large enough for you to get the slippers on your feet after felting.
If there are more than 4 sts between color changes, twist the yarns around each other every 3 to 4 stitches to avoid long floats.
Don't forget to alternate two strands of yarn on every stitch throughout.
For additional details about knitting the slippers, refer to Chapter 3, Basic Slippers, pages 15-19.

Every stitch brings out the same excitement, and, when the resulting product is good, you'll want to knit more slippers the same way!

With circular and one strand of Blue, CO 72 sts; join, being careful not to twist cast-on row. Join second strand of Blue and work following the chart until 1 row remains; the first row of chart = cast-on row.

On the last rnd of the charted pattern (the Blue round), decrease evenly spaced around as follows:
SIZE S: decrease 16 sts to 56 sts total
SIZE M: decrease 12 sts to 60 sts total
SIZE L: decrease 8 sts to 64 sts total.
Continue to the heel and heel shaping with Blue, alternating the two strands on every stitch.

HEEL

ROW 1: K14 (15, 16), knitting last st with both strands; turn.
ROW 2: Sl 1, p27 (29, 31), purling last st with both strands; turn.
Work another 11 rows in stockinette over the 28 (30, 32) heel sts, always slipping the first st.

HEEL TURN

ROW 14: P13 (15, 17), p2tog, p1 with both strands; turn.
ROW 15: K3 (5, 7), k2tog, k1 with both strands; turn.
ROWS 16-23: Continue in stockinette and shaping, with 1 more st before the decrease on each row (the decrease joins the sts before/after the gap).
ROW 24: P12 (14, 16), p2tog, p1 with both strands; turn.
ROW 25: K13 (15, 17), k2tog with both strands; turn. (**NOTE:** This row ends with k2tog and not k1 as previously.)
ROW 26: P13 (15, 17), p2tog, p1 with both strands; turn.

FOOT

SET-UP RND: Ssk, k6 (7, 8). Pm at center of sole, k7 (8, 9), pick up and knit 7 sts evenly spaced across one side of the heel flap, k28 (30, 32) across instep, pick up and knit 7 sts evenly spaced across other side of heel flap and k7 (8, 9) on sole. The beginning of the rnd is at center of sole.
FOOT: Knit 33 (36, 39) rnds on the 56 (60, 64) sts of foot. Divide the sts onto 4 dpn with 14 (15, 16) sts on each needle. Shape toe as follows, with 8 sts decreased on each decrease rnd.
RND 1 (DECREASE RND): At beginning of each needle: K1, k2tog. At end of each needle: K2tog, k1.
RND 2: Knit.
Repeat Rnds 1-2 until 16 (20, 16) sts rem. Cut yarn and draw end through remaining sts. Pull tight and weave in all ends neatly on WS. Steam press and then felt slippers.

BONN
ERS
månadstidning
nr 2 1952
Sport & rese-
garderoben

Slippers from Sør-Varanger

We found this pattern in the book *Sami Handcrafts in Finnmark*. The panel was originally used as a woven edging for cardigans on a women's sweater from Sør-Varanger. Tassels decorated the Sami *skaller* (moccasins). Our slippers are embellished with large pompoms inspired by the pompom on the Sami-themed front page of Bonnier's monthly magazine from 1952.

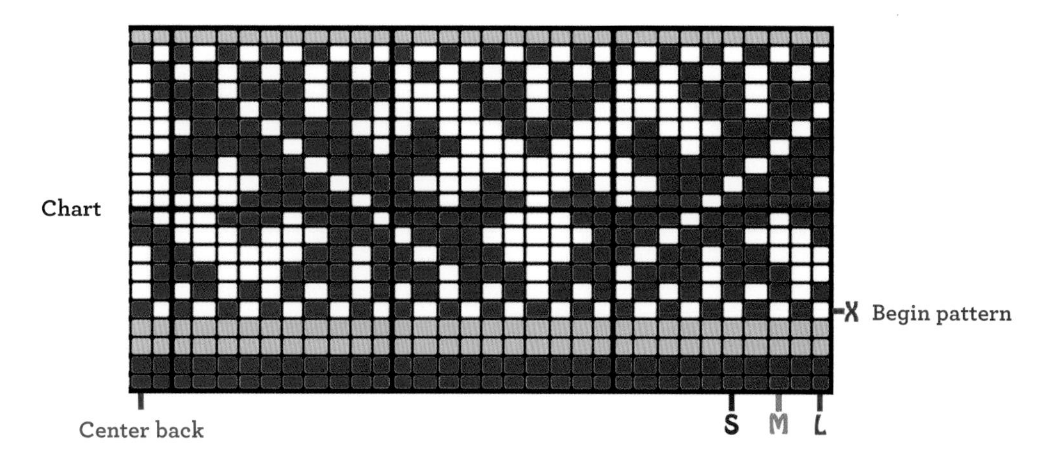

MATERIALS

Yarn: Rauma Vamsegarn (CYCA #4, worsted/afghan/aran; 100% wool; 91 yd/83 m / 50 g)
2-3 balls Gray Heather V13
1 ball Red V18
1 ball Yellow V25
1 ball Off-White V01

Needles: U.S. size 8-10 / 5-6 mm: circular and set of 5 dpn

Recommended Gauge: 14-16 sts = 4 in / 10 cm

NOTES

If there are more than 4 sts between color changes, twist the yarns around each other every 3 to 4 stitches to avoid long floats.
Don't forget to alternate two strands of yarn on every stitch throughout.
For additional details about knitting the slippers, refer to Chapter 3, Basic Slippers, pages 15-19.

With 1 strand of Red and circular, CO 55 (59, 63) sts. Add second strand of Red and work back and forth as follows:

Row 1, with Red: K55 (59, 63), alternating the 2 strands on every stitch; knit last st with both strands; turn.
Row 2, with Yellow: K55 (59, 63), alternating the 2 strands on every stitch; knit last st with both strands; turn.
Row 3, with Yellow: K55 (59, 63), alternating the 2 strands on every stitch; knit last st with both strands; turn.
Row 4: Begin on the chart row marked X, at the stitch for your size.
Rows 5-18: Continue following the chart, working back and forth in stockinette, beginning with a purl row (= Row 5).
Rnd 19, with Yellow: Join to work in the round: K55 (59, 63), alternating two strands around. Increase in the last st = 56 (60, 64) sts. Now k28 (30, 32) to center back; pm (*round now begins at center back*).
Rnd 20, with Yellow: Purl around.
Rnd 21, with Gray Heather: Knit around.
Turn the slipper inside out and knit 6 rnds with Gray Heather. Now work the heel as follows (make sure you use the correct stitch count for your size):

You can buy a pompom maker at hobby shops or make your own. Cut two circles with a hole at the center out of card-stock. Hold the two rings together and wrap the yarn around. Cut open between the two circles; tie a spare length of yarn as tightly as possible around the cut yarn where it passes between the two circles before removing the circles. Our large pompoms have a diameter of 3½ in / 9 cm as measured from outer edge to outer edge. The small pompoms measure 2¼ in / 5.5 cm across.

HEEL

Always slip the first st of the row when working back and forth.

Row 1: K14 (15, 16), knitting last st with both strands; turn.

Row 2: Sl 1, p27 (29, 31), purling last st with both strands; turn.

Work another 11 rows back and forth in stockinette over the 28 (30, 32) heel sts, always slipping the first st.

HEEL TURN

Row 14: P13 (15, 17), p2tog, p1 with both strands; turn.

Row 15: K3 (5, 7), k2tog, k1 with both strands; turn.

Rows 16-23: Continue in stockinette and shaping, with 1 more st before the decrease on each row (the decrease joins the sts before/after the gap).

Row 24: P12 (14, 16), p2tog, p1 with both strands; turn.

Row 25: K13 (15, 17), k2tog with both strands; turn. (**NOTE:** This row ends with k2tog and not k1 as previously.)

Row 26: P13 (15, 17), p2tog, p1 with both strands; turn.

FOOT

Set-up Rnd: Ssk, k6 (7, 8). Pm at center of sole, k7 (8, 9), pick up and knit 7 sts evenly spaced across one side of the heel flap, k28 (30, 32) across instep, pick up and knit 7 sts evenly spaced across other side of heel flap and k7 (8, 9) on sole. The beginning of the rnd is at center of sole.

Foot: Knit 33 (36, 39) rnds on the 56 (60, 64) sts of foot. Divide the sts onto 4 dpn with 14 (15, 16) sts on each needle. Shape toe as follows, with 8 sts decreased on each decrease rnd.

Rnd 1 (decrease rnd): At beginning of each needle: K1, k2tog. At end of each needle: K2tog, k1.

Rnd 2: Knit.

Repeat Rnds 1-2 until 16 (20, 16) sts rem. Cut yarn and draw end through remaining sts. Pull tight and weave in all ends neatly on WS.

FINISHING

Steam press and then felt slippers.

Make a large pompom with Red, Off-White, and Yellow for each slipper. Sew pompom securely to top of center front.

Chevron pattern slippers

These slippers were inspired by the bands used to decorate Sami costumes. The bright colors should put you in a good mood, so save these slippers to wear on cold gray days!

MATERIALS

Yarn: Rauma Vamsegarn (CYCA #4, worsted/afghan/aran; 100% wool; 91 yd/83 m / 50 g)
1-2 balls Dark Brown Heather V64
1 ball Yellow V25
1 ball Bright Pink V56

Needles: U.S. size 8-10 / 5-6 mm: circular and set of 5 dpn

Recommended Gauge: 14-16 sts = 4 in / 10 cm

NOTES

If there are more than 4 sts between color changes, twist the yarns around each other every 3 to 4 stitches to avoid long floats.
Don't forget to alternate two strands of yarn on every stitch throughout.
For additional details about knitting the slippers, refer to Chapter 3, Basic Slippers, pages 15-19.

With one strand of Yellow and circular, CO 55 (59, 63) sts; join, being careful not to twist cast-on row. Join second strand of Yellow and work following the chart (the first row of the chart = cast-on row), alternating two strands of yarn on each stitch. On last rnd of chart, increase 1 st at end of rnd = 56 (60, 64) sts.

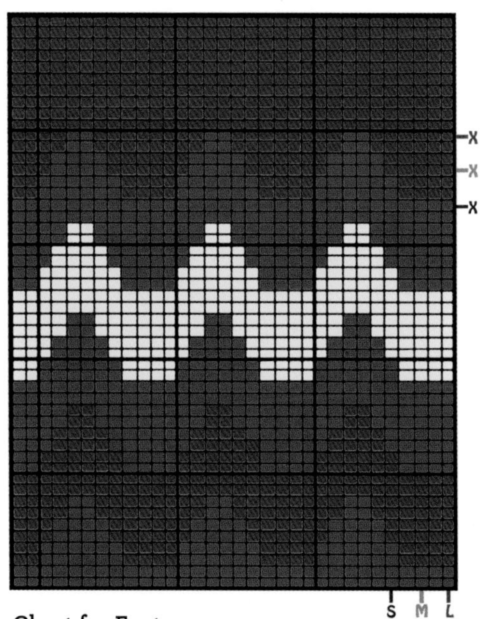

Chart for Foot

At the X corresponding to the appropriate size, begin decreasing for the toe.

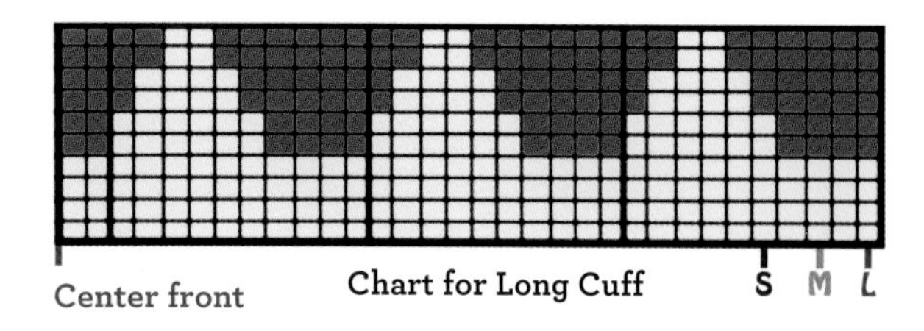

Chart for Long Cuff

Continue with two strands of Dark Brown Heather, working heel as follows:

HEEL

Row 1: K14 (15, 16), knitting last st with both strands; turn.
Row 2: Sl 1, p27 (29, 31), purling last st with both strands; turn.
Work another 11 rows back and forth in stockinette over the 28 (30, 32) heel sts, always slipping the first st.

HEEL TURN

Row 14: P13 (15, 17), p2tog, p1 with both strands; turn.
Row 15: K3 (5, 7), k2tog, k1 with both strands; turn.
Rows 16-23: Continue the same way, working back and forth in stockinette and shaping, with 1 more st before the decrease on each row (the decrease joins the sts before/after the gap).
Row 24: P12 (14, 16), p2tog, p1 with both strands; turn.
Row 25: K13 (15, 17), k2tog with both strands; turn. (**NOTE:** This row ends with k2tog and not k1 as previously.)
Row 26: P13 (15, 17), p2tog, p1 with both strands; turn.

FOOT

Set-up Rnd, with Dark Brown Heather: Ssk, k6 (7, 8). Pm at center of sole, k7 (8, 9), pick up and knit 7 sts evenly spaced across one side of the heel flap, k28 (30, 32) across instep, pick up and knit 7 sts evenly spaced across other side of heel flap and k7 (8, 9) on sole. The beginning of the rnd is at center of sole.
Foot: Working in charted pattern for foot, knit 33 (36, 39) rnds on the 56 (60, 64) sts of foot.
Divide the sts onto 4 dpn with 14 (15, 16) sts on each needle. With Bright Pink only, shape toe as follows, with 8 sts decreased on each decrease rnd.
Rnd 1 (decrease rnd): At beginning of each needle: K1, k2tog. At end of each needle: K2tog, k1.
Rnd 2: Knit.
Repeat Rnds 1-2 until 16 (20, 16) sts rem. Cut yarn and draw end through remaining sts. Pull tight and weave in all ends neatly on WS. Steam press and then felt slippers.

Slippers with embroidered reindeer

These reindeer figures were inspired by reindeer we saw on a picture of a drum from Finnmark that had been confiscated from the Sami in 1691. The reindeer are embroidered on the slippers after they have been felted.

Reindeer are considered an Arctic animal and, for most of the year, roam the tundra and northern mountain landscape through the large conifer forest belt stretching across Europe, Asia, and America. One can certainly say that this forest belt is their primary habitat. The mountain and tundra reindeer wander from the northern edge of the forest lands northwards to the treeless lands, to the tundra, or to the high mountains and coastlands. The forest reindeer roam from the deep forests to the high-lying and treeless regions of the large mountain chains that run through the forest lands such as Siberia and Alaska or to the mountain ridges that barely rise above the forests, such as in the Finnish regions.

OTTAR, POPULAR PAMPHLETS FROM THE TROMSØ MUSEUM, JUNE 1958

MATERIALS

YARN: Rauma Vamsegarn (CYCA #4, worsted/afghan/aran; 100% wool; 91 yd/83 m / 50 g)
3-4 balls Dark Brown Heather V64

NOTIONS: Embroidery thread: DMC Red 666
Aida fabric 352, waste canvas

NEEDLES: U.S. size 8-10 / 5-6 mm: circular and set of 5 dpn

RECOMMENDED GAUGE: 14-16 sts = 4 in / 10 cm

NOTES

Don't forget to alternate two strands of yarn on every stitch throughout.
For additional details about knitting the slippers, refer to Chapter 3, Basic Slippers, pages 15-19.

With one strand of Dark Brown Heather and circular, CO 56 (60, 64) sts; join, being careful not to twist cast-on row. Join second strand of Dark Brown Heather and work 20 rnds in stockinette.

HEEL

ROW 1: K14 (15, 16), knitting last st with both strands; turn.
ROW 2: Sl 1, p27 (29, 31), purling last st with both strands; turn.
Work another 11 rows back and forth in stockinette over the 28 (30, 32) heel sts, always slipping the first st.

HEEL TURN

ROW 14: P13 (15, 17), p2tog, p1 with both strands; turn.
ROW 15: K3 (5, 7), k2tog, k1 with both strands; turn.
ROWS 16-23: Continue the same way, working back and forth in stockinette and shaping, with 1 more st before the decrease on each row (the decrease joins the sts before/after the gap).
ROW 24: P12 (14, 16), p2tog, p1 with both strands; turn.
ROW 25: K13 (15, 17), k2tog with both strands; turn.
(**NOTE:** This row ends with k2tog and not k1 as previously.)
ROW 26: P13 (15, 17), p2tog, p1 with both strands; turn.

FOOT

SET-UP RND: Ssk, k6 (7, 8). Pm at center of sole, k7 (8, 9), pick up and knit 7 sts evenly spaced across one side of the heel flap, k28 (30, 32) across instep, pick up and knit 7 sts evenly spaced across other side of heel flap and k7 (8, 9) on sole. The beginning of the rnd is at center of sole.

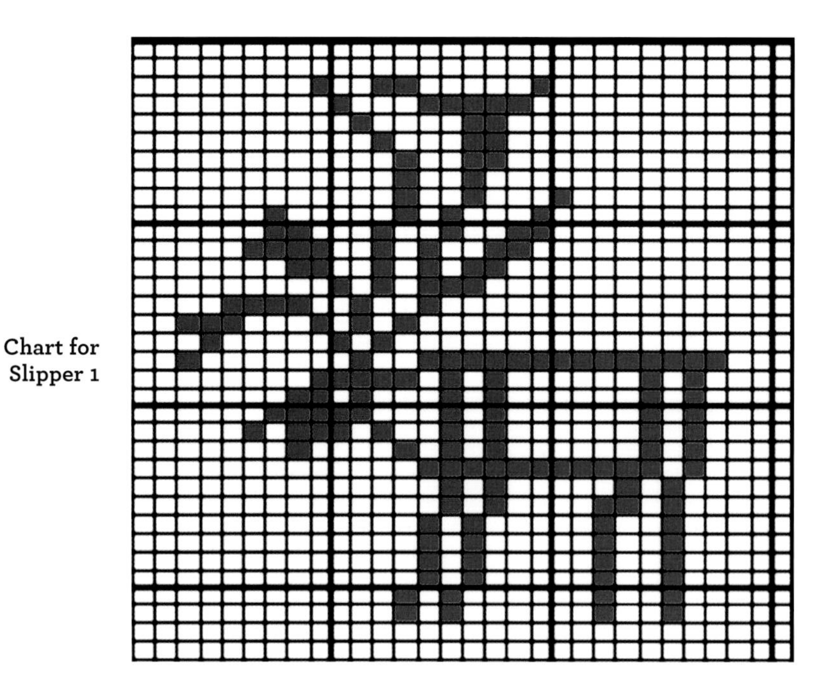

Chart for Slipper 1

Foot: Knit 33 (36, 39) rnds on the 56 (60, 64) sts of foot. Divide the sts onto 4 dpn with 14 (15, 16) sts on each needle. Shape toe as follows, with 8 sts decreased on each decrease rnd.

Rnd 1 (decrease rnd): At beginning of each needle: K1, k2tog. At end of each needle: K2tog, k1.

Rnd 2: Knit.

Repeat Rnds 1-2 until 16 (20, 16) sts rem.

Cut yarn and draw end through remaining sts. Pull tight and weave in all ends neatly on WS. Steam press and then felt slippers.

REINDEER MOTIF

Hold the felted and dry slipper with the side facing up and then place the waste canvas over the cuff so that it is aligned horizontally, edge to edge. We began the embroidery 6 holes from the top. Embroider the reindeer motif in cross stitch through the waste canvas and slipper. Make sure that your stitches are even, aligned, and all worked the same way. When each reindeer is complete, carefully remove the strands of the canvas. Use your measuring tape to double check that the reindeer are aligned the same way on each of the slippers.

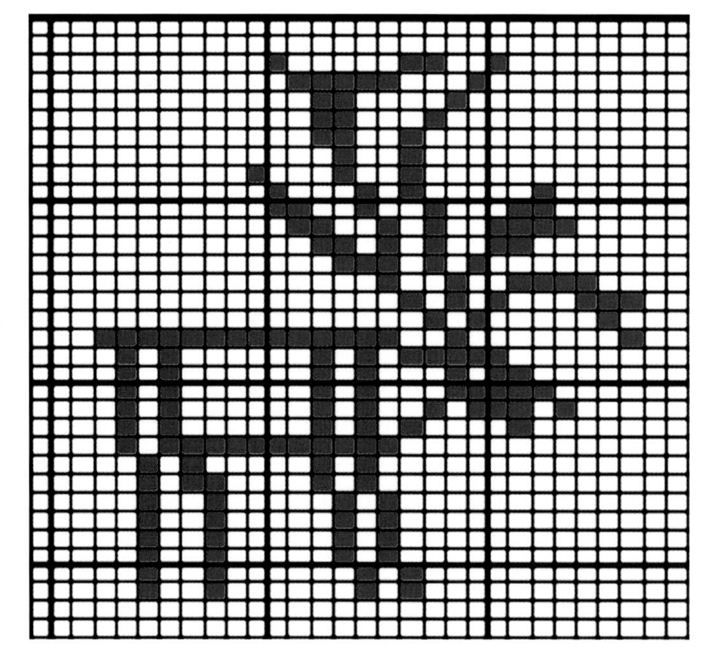

Chart for Slipper 2

Godt nytt år!

Snowball slippers

The idea for these slippers came from the image of a little boy throwing a snowball on a Swedish Christmas card. The ankle has an eyelet row with twisted cords threaded through before felting.

MATERIALS

YARN: Rauma Vamsegarn (CYCA #4, worsted/afghan/aran; 100% wool; 91 yd/83 m / 50 g)
3-4 balls Olive Green V89
1 ball Bright Pink V56
1 ball Yellow V25
1 ball Bright Navy Blue V67
1 ball Off-White V01

NEEDLES: U.S. size 8-10 / 5-6 mm: circular and set of 5 dpn

RECOMMENDED GAUGE: 14-16 sts = 4 in / 10 cm

NOTES

Don't forget to alternate two strands of yarn on every stitch throughout.
For additional details about knitting the slippers, refer to Chapter 3, Basic Slippers, pages 15-19.

With one strand of Bright Pink and circular, CO 56 (60, 64) sts; join, being careful not to twist cast-on row. Join second strand of Bright Pink and knit 1 rnd.
EYELET RND: With one strand of Bright Pink, work (k2tog, yo) around.
With two strands of Bright Pink alternating on each stitch, knit 3 rnds.
Change to Olive Green and work heel as follows:

HEEL

ROW 1: K14 (15, 16), knitting last st with both strands; turn.
ROW 2: Sl 1, p27 (29, 31), purling last st with both strands; turn.
Work another 11 rows back and forth in stockinette over the 28 (30, 32) heel sts, always slipping the first st.

HEEL TURN

ROW 14: P13 (15, 17), p2tog, p1 with both strands; turn.
ROW 15: K3 (5, 7), k2tog, k1 with both strands; turn.
ROWS 16-23: Continue the same way, working back and forth in stockinette and shaping, with 1 more st before the decrease on each row (the decrease joins the sts before/after the gap).
ROW 24: P12 (14, 16), p2tog, p1 with both strands; turn.
ROW 25: K13 (15, 17), k2tog with both strands; turn. (**NOTE:** This row ends with k2tog and not k1 as previously.)
ROW 26: P13 (15, 17), p2tog, p1 with both strands; turn.

FOOT

SET-UP RND: Ssk, k6 (7, 8). Pm at center of sole, k7 (8, 9), pick up and knit 7 sts evenly spaced across one side of the heel flap, k28 (30, 32) across instep, pick up and knit 7 sts evenly spaced across other side of heel flap and k7 (8, 9) on sole. The beginning of the rnd is at center of sole.
FOOT: Knit 33 (36, 39) rnds on the 56 (60, 64) sts of foot. Divide the sts onto 4 dpn with 14 (15, 16) sts on each needle. Shape toe as follows, with 8 sts decreased on each decrease rnd.
RND 1 (DECREASE RND): At beginning of each needle: K1, k2tog. At end of each needle: K2tog, k1.
RND 2: Knit.
Repeat Rnds 1-2 until 16 (20, 16) sts rem. Cut yarn and draw end through remaining sts. Pull tight and weave in all ends neatly on WS.

FINISHING

Steam press slippers.
MAKE 2 CORDS: Cut 2 strands each (about 120 in / 300 cm long) of Blue, Yellow, and White yarn. Twist strands into a cord 40 in / 100 cm long and thread through the eyelet rnds of each slipper. Begin threading at center back and end at the center front hole (size Medium has two holes at center front).
Felt the slippers with the cords in place. Make two 3½ in / 9 cm diameter pompoms for each slipper. Attach pompoms very securely to ends of cords.

Chapter 6

Native American moccasins

I always wanted to be an Indian when I grew up and it was only when I was a bit older that I discovered it was not something one could become. I went to school early on Tuesdays, magazine delivery days, and stood outside the shop until it opened. I then waited until the shop clerk wheeled in the handcart with the new weeklies. She found the bundle with *The Silver Arrow*, carefully removed the plastic, and, as usual, gave the first copy to me.

When the snow melted in the spring, the camp in Svendsrud Forest was set up. The tipi was raised and the totem pole decorated. Let war or the hunt begin! Large moss-covered stones were buffalo and these were skinned and the skin taken back to camp. Too bad for anyone who wandered into Svendsrud Forest! If the intruder was a schoolboy, he could end up tied to the totem pole with little Indians in their regalia dancing around to the beat of the drum-sticks on Grandmother's old cooking pot.

Arne's childhood memories from Svendsrud Forest.

Arapaho slippers

Slippers with high cuffs and patterns influenced by traditional motifs used by the Arapaho tribe. The inspiration for the patterning on this pair was found in the book *The Native Americans.*

MATERIALS

YARN: Rauma Vamsegarn (CYCA #4, worsted/afghan/aran; 100% wool; 91 yd/83 m / 50 g)
2 balls Bright Royal Blue V37
2 balls Warm Beige V05
1 ball Lilac V96
1 ball Evergreen V88
1 ball Red V18

NEEDLES: U.S. size 8-10 / 5-6 mm: circular and set of 5 dpn

RECOMMENDED GAUGE: 14-16 sts = 4 in / 10 cm

NOTES

All sizes begin with the same stitch count so the cuff will be large enough for you to get the slippers on your feet after felting.
Don't forget to alternate two strands of yarn on every stitch throughout.
For additional details about knitting the slippers, refer to Chapter 3, Basic Slippers, pages 15-19.

With one strand of Blue and circular, CO 64 sts; join, being careful not to twist cast-on row. Join second strand of Blue and work following the chart. Note that the first row of the chart = cast-on row.
On the last rnd (Row 34 of chart), work alternating the 2 strands of Blue and decrease evenly spaced around as follows:
SIZE S: decrease 8 sts = 56 sts rem
SIZE M: decrease 4 sts = 60 sts rem
SIZE L: decrease 0 sts = 64 sts rem

HEEL

Work the heel with Blue as follows:
ROW 1: K14 (15, 16), knitting last st with both strands; turn.
ROW 2: Sl 1, p27 (29, 31), purling last st with both strands; turn.
Work another 11 rows back and forth in stockinette over the 28 (30, 32) heel sts, always slipping the first st.

HEEL TURN

ROW 14: P13 (15, 17), p2tog, p1 with both strands; turn.
ROW 15: K3 (5, 7), k2tog, k1 with both strands; turn.
ROWS 16-23: Continue the same way, working back and forth in stockinette and shaping, with 1 more st before the decrease on each row (the decrease joins the sts before/after the gap).
ROW 24: P12 (14, 16), p2tog, p1 with both strands; turn.
ROW 25: K13 (15, 17), k2tog with both strands; turn.
(**NOTE:** This row ends with k2tog and not k1 as previously.)
ROW 26: P13 (15, 17), p2tog, p1 with both strands; turn.

FOOT

SET-UP RND: Ssk, k6 (7, 8). Pm at center of sole, k7 (8, 9), pick up and knit 7 sts evenly spaced across one side of the heel flap, k28 (30, 32) across instep, pick up and knit 7 sts evenly spaced across other side of heel flap and k7 (8, 9) on sole. The beginning of the rnd is at center of sole.
FOOT: Following the chart for the foot and beginning at the marker for your size, knit 33 (36, 39) rnds on the 56 (60, 64) sts of foot.
Divide the sts onto 4 dpn with 14 (15, 16) sts on each needle. With Blue only, shape toe as follows, with 8 sts decreased on each decrease rnd.
RND 1 (DECREASE RND): At beginning of each needle: K1, k2tog. At end of each needle: K2tog, k1.
RND 2: Knit.
Repeat Rnds 1-2 until 16 (20, 16) sts rem. Cut yarn and draw end through remaining sts. Pull tight and weave in all ends neatly on WS. Steam press and then felt slippers.

Chart for Long Cuff

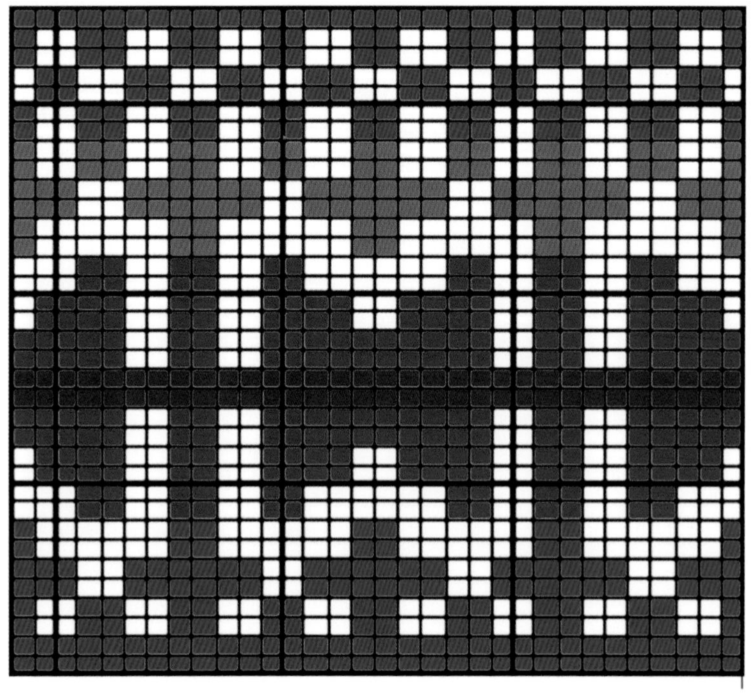

Chart for Foot

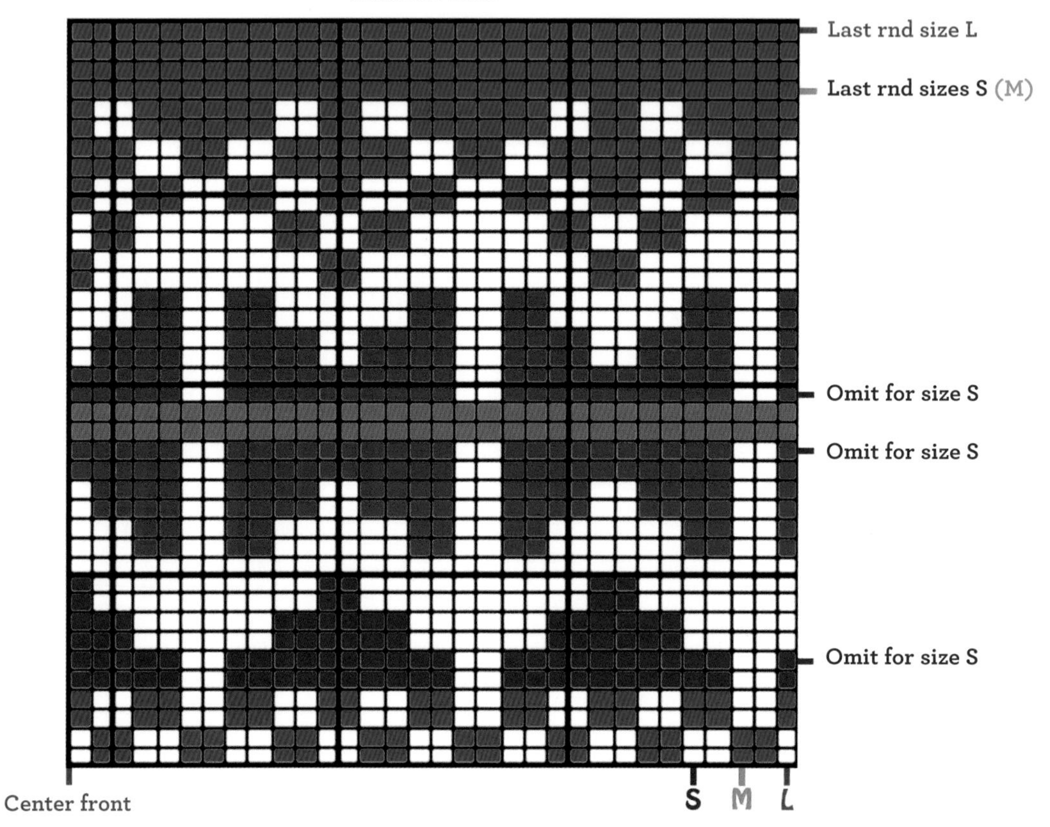

Fringed Sioux slippers

The inspiration for these slippers came from a picture of a Sioux saddlebag. It featured bright bead embroidery against a white background. The embroidery technique with beads on a cord makes a pattern in a technique called "dove stitch." The saddlebag has several rows, one over the other, producing a striped effect. We kept to one stripe for our slippers. Finally we can live out our Indian dreams in our adult life! These slippers are meant for indoor use only. Nothing here is as might be experienced at the tipi in Svendsrud Forest but Arne is inside, fixing fringe and beads that perhaps got ripped off in the fight.

MATERIALS

Yarn: Rauma Vamsegarn (CYCA #4, worsted/afghan/aran; 100% wool; 91 yd/83 m / 50 g), 3-4 balls Rust V42
Rauma Mitu (CYCA #3, DK/light worsted, 50% alpaca, 50% wool; 109 yd/100 m / 50 g), 1 ball Yellow 0184

Notions: Glass seed beads in white, green, yellow, orange, light blue, dark blue, and brown; strong sewing thread (Nymo quilting thread recommended); beading needle, size 9 or 10

Needles: U.S. size 8-10 / 5-6 mm: circular and set of 5 dpn
Crochet Hook: U.S. size E-4 / 3.5 mm

Recommended Gauge: 14-16 sts = 4 in / 10 cm

NOTES

Don't forget to alternate two strands of yarn on every stitch throughout.
For additional details about knitting the slippers, refer to Chapter 3, Basic Slippers, pages 15-19.

With one strand of Rust and circular, CO 56 (60, 64) sts. Join second strand of Rust and knit 10 rows back and forth in garter st, alternating the two strands on every stitch.
Join for a short cuff: Work 28 (30, 32) sts to center back, pm for beginning of rnd, and work 13 rnds.

HEEL

Row 1: K14 (15, 16), knitting last st with both strands; turn.
Row 2: Sl 1, p27 (29, 31), purling last st with both strands; turn.
Work another 11 rows back and forth in stockinette over the 28 (30, 32) heel sts, always slipping the first st.

HEEL TURN

Row 14: P13 (15, 17), p2tog, p1 with both strands; turn.
Row 15: K3 (5, 7), k2tog, k1 with both strands; turn.
Rows 16-23: Continue the same way, working back and forth in stockinette and shaping, with 1 more st before the decrease on each row (the decrease joins the sts before/after the gap).
Row 24: P12 (14, 16), p2tog, p1 with both strands; turn.
Row 25: K13 (15, 17), k2tog with both strands; turn. (**NOTE:** This row ends with k2tog and not k1 as previously.)
Row 26: P13 (15, 17), p2tog, p1 with both strands; turn.

FOOT

Set-up Rnd: Ssk, k6 (7, 8). Pm at center of sole, k7 (8, 9), pick up and knit 7 sts evenly spaced across one side of the heel flap, k28 (30, 32) across instep, pick up and knit 7 sts evenly spaced across other side of heel flap and k7 (8, 9) on sole. The beginning of the rnd is at center of sole.
Foot: Knit 33 (36, 39) rnds on the 56 (60, 64) sts of foot. Divide the sts onto 4 dpn with 14 (15, 16) sts on each needle. Shape toe as follows, with 8 sts decreased on each decrease rnd.
Rnd 1 (decrease rnd): At beginning of each needle: K1, k2tog. At end of each needle: K2tog, k1.
Rnd 2: Knit.
Repeat Rnds 1-2 until 16 (20, 16) sts rem. Cut yarn and draw end through remaining sts. Pull tight and weave in all ends neatly on WS.

FINISHING

Steam press and then felt slippers before decorating them with fringe and beads.

CROCHETED FRINGE

Photo 1: Begin each fringe with a chain.

Photo 2: Crochet back into the chain with 2 sc in each ch, beginning 3rd ch from hook.

Photo 3: Working 2 sc in each ch makes the fringe curl.

FRINGE

Make a crochet chain as long as the length of the cuff of your slipper. Make sure you have a multiple of 3+1 ch. The fringes are worked out from this chain.
Make each fringe as follows: *Ch 18, beginning in 3rd ch from hook, work 2 sc in each ch back to main chain*.
Securely sew the fringes on the underside of the cuff.
Fold cuff down and sew the beads on with dove stitch.

DOVE STITCH

Begin embroidering at the center back by bringing the thread through the cuff on the slipper, directly over the edge with the fringe. Pick up the beads following the chart—for example: 1 white, 2 green, 3 orange, 2 green, 1 white. Sew beaded strand down directly above the hole where the needle came up at base of strand. Align the strands as evenly as possible so that the beads will lie smoothly. We used small and uneven beads from Panduro (a Scandinavian craft shop). Because the beads are not all exactly the same size, they will “dance” a little, but we don’t worry about that. Make a knot with the thread every time you fasten the row.
Finish by balancing the rows of beads by aligning them smoothly side by side and sewing a stitch at the center of the row to hold each row in place.

DOVE STITCH

Photo 1: The collar with the bead embroidery and fringe.

Photo 2: Pick up the beads in the color sequence shown on the chart.

Photo 3: 9 vertical beads, beginning at center back.

Photo 4: Sew on the vertical rows of beads so they lie smoothly side by side.

Photo 5: Carefully tighten the bead strand so it lies smoothly beside the previous strand.

Photo 6: Make a knot on the back before you sew on the next row.

Photo 7: If the beads are uneven, you can balance the motif and sew an extra stitch in the center of the row to align the motif.

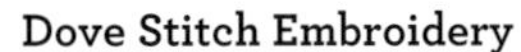

Dove Stitch Embroidery

Center back

Chippewa
Early 19th Century
Northeastern Woodland
Menominee
Early 19th Century
Northeastern Woodland

Moccasin slippers with crocheted fringe and embroidery

These slippers are knitted following the basic pattern and then decorated with crocheted fringe and embroidery. The colors and designs are taken from an old paper-doll book. We first saw the crocheted fringe that we used for these and the previous slippers in the reception area of a small hotel near the Pompidou Centre in Paris. The hotel was managed by an old woman from Portugal who was happy that Carlos spoke Portuguese and, not least, that we were interested in her crochet. The lobby was full of tablecloths, runners, and tray covers, all her own work. A runner with this fine fringe lay over a chest of drawers behind the front desk. She gave us a quick introduction to making the fringe. We then headed for the nearest yarn shop so we could crochet while the lesson was still fresh in our minds.

MATERIALS

YARN: Rauma Vamsegarn (CYCA #4, worsted/afghan/aran; 100% wool; 91 yd/83 m / 50 g)
2-3 balls Light Gray Heather V03
1 ball Bright Royal Blue V37
1 ball Evergreen V88
1 ball Red V18
1 ball Yellow V25

NEEDLES: U.S. size 8-10 / 5-6 mm: circular and set of 5 dpn

CROCHET HOOK: between U.S. size H-8 and J-10 / 5 and 6 mm

RECOMMENDED GAUGE: 14-16 sts = 4 in / 10 cm

NOTES

Don't forget to alternate two strands of yarn on every stitch throughout.
For additional details about knitting the slippers, refer to Chapter 3, Basic Slippers, pages 15-19.

With one strand of Light Gray Heather and circular, CO 56 (60, 64) sts; join, being careful not to twist cast-on row. Join second strand of Light Gray Heather and knit 3 rnds, alternating strands on every stitch.

HEEL

ROW 1: K14 (15, 16), knitting last st with both strands; turn.
ROW 2: Sl 1, p27 (29, 31), purling last st with both strands; turn.
Work another 11 rows back and forth in stockinette over the 28 (30, 32) heel sts, always slipping the first st.

HEEL TURN

ROW 14: P13 (15, 17), p2tog, p1 with both strands; turn.
ROW 15: K3 (5, 7), k2tog, k1 with both strands; turn.
ROWS 16-23: Continue the same way, working back and forth in stockinette and shaping, with 1 more st before the decrease on each row (the decrease joins the sts before/after the gap).
ROW 24: P12 (14, 16), p2tog, p1 with both strands; turn.

Embroidery Chart

Row 25: K13 (15, 17), k2tog with both strands; turn. (**NOTE:** This row ends with k2tog and not k1 as previously.)
Row 26: P13 (15, 17), p2tog, p1 with both strands; turn.

FOOT

Set-up Rnd: Ssk, k6 (7, 8). Pm at center of sole, k7 (8, 9), pick up and knit 7 sts evenly spaced across one side of the heel flap, k28 (30, 32) across instep, pick up and knit 7 sts evenly spaced across other side of heel flap and k7 (8, 9) on sole. The beginning of the rnd is at center of sole.
Foot: Knit 33 (36, 39) rnds on the 56 (60, 64) sts of foot. Divide the sts onto 4 dpn with 14 (15, 16) sts on each needle. Shape toe as follows, with 8 sts decreased on each decrease rnd.
Rnd 1 (decrease rnd): At beginning of each needle: K1, k2tog. At end of each needle: K2tog, k1.
Rnd 2: Knit.
Repeat Rnds 1-2 until 16 (20, 16) sts rem. Cut yarn and draw end through remaining sts. Pull tight and weave in all ends neatly on WS.

FINISHING

Steam press slippers.
Edging: Work single crochet around the ankle.
Fringe: Work *1 sc, ch 14, beginning in 3rd ch from hook, work 2 sc in each chain.
Work 1 sc each in the 1st and 2nd edge sts at base of fringe.*
Repeat from * to * around.
Embroider the charted motif, beginning at center front in the 4th st from the crocheted edge.
Steam press the embroidery and then felt slippers.

Fun American Indian slippers in the boys' room—for anyone who wanted to be an Indian when they grew up.

Slippers with a pattern from an old scrapbook

We sketched out this pattern in 2007, inspired by a design found in a calendar with drawings of traditional dress from various cultures, including American Indians. That pattern was never used, but we were able to recycle it for this slipper design—an example of why you should never throw anything away.

Chart for Long Cuff

Center front

MATERIALS

Yarn: Rauma Vamsegarn (CYCA #4, worsted/afghan/aran; 100% wool; 91 yd/83 m / 50 g)
2 balls Dark Brown Heather V64
2 balls Red V18
1 ball Spring Green V45
1 ball Light Blue V50
1 ball Off-White V01
1 ball Bright Yellow V26

Needles: U.S. size 8-10 / 5-6 mm: circular and set of 5 dpn

Recommended Gauge: 14-16 sts = 4 in / 10 cm

NOTES

Don't forget to alternate two strands of yarn on every stitch throughout.
For additional details about knitting the slippers, refer to Chapter 3, Basic Slippers, pages 15-19.

With one strand of Dark Brown Heather and circular, CO 56 (60, 64) sts; join, being careful not to twist cast-on row.

Join second strand of Dark Brown Heather and begin following the chart at the marker for your size—the first row of the chart = cast-on row.

HEEL

Work the heel with two strands of Red, alternating strands on every stitch.
Row 1: K14 (15, 16), knitting last st with both strands; turn.
Row 2: Sl 1, p27 (29, 31), purling last st with both strands; turn.
Work another 11 rows back and forth in stockinette over the 28 (30, 32) heel sts, always slipping the first st.

HEEL TURN

Row 14: P13 (15, 17), p2tog, p1 with both strands; turn.
Row 15: K3 (5, 7), k2tog, k1 with both strands; turn.
Rows 16-23: Continue the same way, working back and forth in stockinette and shaping, with 1 more st before the decrease on each row (the decrease joins the sts before/after the gap).
Row 24: P12 (14, 16), p2tog, p1 with both strands; turn.

Chart for Foot

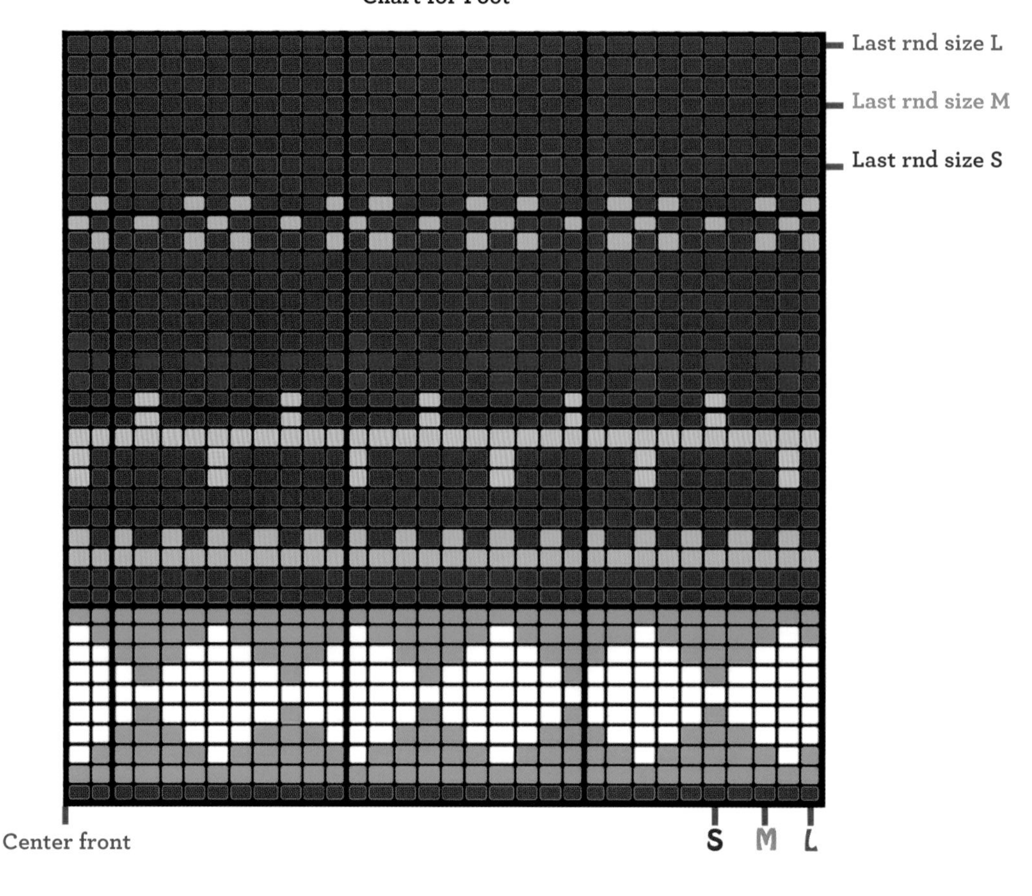

Row 25: K13 (15, 17), k2tog with both strands; turn. (**NOTE:** This row ends with k2tog and not k1 as previously.)
Row 26: P13 (15, 17), p2tog, p1 with both strands; turn.

FOOT
Set-up Rnd: Ssk, k6 (7, 8). Pm at center of sole, k7 (8, 9), pick up and knit 7 sts evenly spaced across one side of the heel flap, k28 (30, 32) across instep, pick up and knit 7 sts evenly spaced across other side of heel flap and k7 (8, 9) on sole. The beginning of the rnd is at center of sole.

Foot: Following the chart for foot and beginning at marker for your size, knit 33 (36, 39) rnds on the 56 (60, 64) sts of foot.
Divide the sts onto 4 dpn with 14 (15, 16) sts on each needle. With Dark Brown Heather only, shape toe as follows, with 8 sts decreased on each decrease rnd.
Rnd 1 (decrease rnd): At beginning of each needle: K1, k2tog. At end of each needle: K2tog, k1.
Rnd 2: Knit.
Repeat Rnds 1-2 until 16 (20, 16) sts rem. Cut yarn and draw end through remaining sts. Pull tight and weave in all ends neatly on WS. Steam press and then felt slippers.

Slippers with horses

These sweet slippers are embroidered with horses with strands of beads for the mane and tail. The perfect gift for every horse-crazy girl!

MATERIALS

Yarn: Rauma Vamsegarn (CYCA #4, worsted/afghan/aran; 100% wool; 91 yd/83 m / 50 g)
3-4 balls Light Blue V49
1 ball Deep Rose Pink V44
1 ball Dark Brown Heather V64

Needles: U.S. size 8-10 / 5-6 mm: circular and set of 5 dpn

Notions: Glass seed beads, about 250; beading needle size 9 or 10; quilting thread

Recommended Gauge: 14-16 sts = 4 in / 10 cm

NOTES

All sizes begin with the same stitch count so the cuff will be large enough for you to get the slippers on your feet after felting.
Don't forget to alternate two strands of yarn on every stitch throughout.
For additional details about knitting the slippers, refer to Chapter 3, Basic Slippers, pages 15-19.

With one strand of Deep Rose Pink and circular, CO 64 sts; join, being careful not to twist cast-on row. Join second strand of Deep Rose Pink and knit 1 rnd. Change to Light Blue and knit 22 rnds, alternating the two strands on every stitch.
Rnd 23: Work alternating the 2 strands of Light Blue, decreasing evenly spaced around as follows:
Size S: decrease 8 sts = 56 sts rem
Size M: decease 4 sts = 60 sts rem
Size L: decrease 0 sts = 64 sts rem

HEEL

Continue working with two strands of Light Blue as follows:
Row 1: K14 (15, 16), knitting last st with both strands; turn.
Row 2: Sl 1, p27 (29, 31), purling last st with both strands; turn.
Work another 11 rows back and forth in stockinette over the 28 (30, 32) heel sts, always slipping the first st.

HEEL TURN

Row 14: P13 (15, 17), p2tog, p1 with both strands; turn.
Row 15: K3 (5, 7), k2tog, k1 with both strands; turn.
Rows 16-23: Continue the same way, working back and forth in stockinette and shaping, with 1 more st before the decrease on each row (the decrease joins the sts before/after the gap).
Row 24: P12 (14, 16), p2tog, p1 with both strands; turn.
Row 25: K13 (15, 17), k2tog with both strands; turn.
(**NOTE:** This row ends with k2tog and not k1 as previously.)
Row 26: P13 (15, 17), p2tog, p1 with both strands; turn.

FOOT

Set-up Rnd: Ssk, k6 (7, 8). Pm at center of sole, k7 (8, 9), pick up and knit 7 sts evenly spaced across one side of the heel flap, k28 (30, 32) across instep, pick up and knit 7 sts evenly spaced across other side of heel flap and k7 (8, 9) on sole. The beginning of the rnd is at center of sole.
Foot: Knit 33 (36, 39) rnds on the 56 (60, 64) sts of foot. Divide the sts onto 4 dpn with 14 (15, 16) sts on each needle. Shape toe as follows, with 8 sts decreased on each decrease rnd.
Rnd 1 (decrease rnd): At beginning of each needle: K1, k2tog. At end of each needle: K2tog, k1.
Rnd 2: Knit.
Repeat Rnds 1-2 until 16 (20, 16) sts rem. Cut yarn and draw end through remaining sts. Pull tight and weave in all ends neatly on WS.

FINISHING

Steam press slippers.
Lay the slipper flat and mark the center front. Embroider the horses with duplicate stitch, following the chart.
Felt slippers and then add beads.

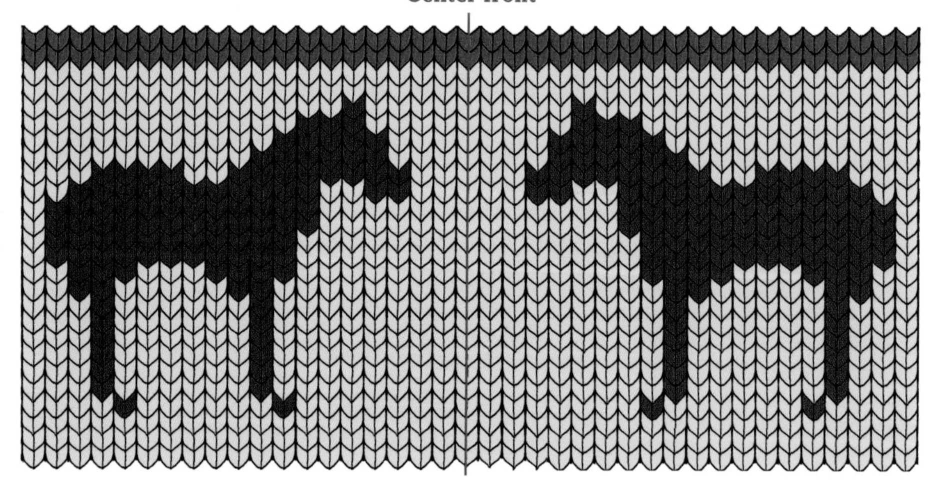

BEADS

Photo 1: Decide how long you want the mane and tail and string on the beads—for example, 13 beads for the mane.

Photo 2: Insert the needle back through the first 12 beads.

Photo 3: Insert the needle down where you came up and make a knot on the WS before you begin the next strand of beads.

Decorating with beads in your choice of color:
MANE: String 13 beads of your color choice onto the quilting thread. Bring the needle back through the first 12 beads on the thread and sew it, securing to WS where the thread emerged previously. Our horses have 13 strands in the mane.
TAIL: 20 beads per strand, 4 strands.

Chapter 7

On the terrace

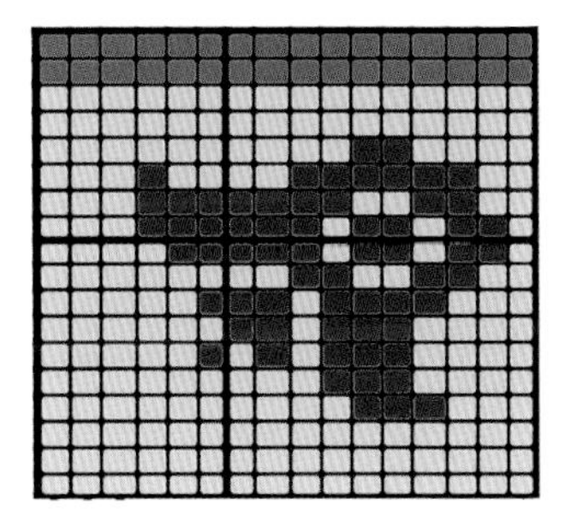

Our flowers are a huge source of inspiration with an endless number of fun motifs to choose from. So, of course, we must write a chapter for the terrace. These slippers can be worn when you water the flowers or go out on the balcony on a cold spring day. But, of course, they are just as nice for indoors.

18

Magnus the garden mouse slippers

These slippers were inspired by Magnus the Field Mouse from our fourth book, *Knit-and-Crochet Garden.* You'll find the pattern for the mouse there. You can knit the slippers with a green toe tip and then embroider on Magnus with duplicate stitch.

MATERIALS

Yarn: Rauma Vamsegarn (CYCA #4, worsted/afghan/aran; 100% wool; 91 yd/83 m / 50 g)
3-4 balls Bright Royal Blue V37
1 ball Spring Green V45
1 ball Gray Heather V13
1 ball Clover Pink V65
1 ball Lilac V96
1 ball Ebony V10

Needles: U.S. size 8-10 / 5-6 mm: circular and set of 5 dpn

Recommended Gauge: 14-16 sts = 4 in / 10 cm

NOTES

Don't forget to alternate two strands of yarn on every stitch throughout.
For additional details about knitting the slippers, refer to Chapter 3, Basic Slippers, pages 15-19.

With one strand of Spring Green and circular, CO 56 (60, 64) sts; join, being careful not to twist cast-on row. Join second strand of Spring Green and knit 2 rnds, alternating the two strands on every stitch. Cut Spring Green and join 2 strands of Bright Royal Blue; knit 2 rnds. Work rest of slipper with Bright Royal Blue.

HEEL

Row 1: K14 (15, 16), knitting last st with both strands; turn.
Row 2: Sl 1, p27 (29, 31), purling last st with both strands; turn.
Work another 11 rows back and forth in stockinette over the 28 (30, 32) heel sts, always slipping the first st.

HEEL TURN

Row 14: P13 (15, 17), p2tog, p1 with both strands; turn.
Row 15: K3 (5, 7), k2tog, k1 with both strands; turn.
Rows 16-23: Continue the same way, working back and forth in stockinette and shaping, with 1 more st before the decrease on each row (the decrease joins the sts before/after the gap).
Row 24: P12 (14, 16), p2tog, p1 with both strands; turn.
Row 25: K13 (15, 17), k2tog with both strands; turn.
(**NOTE:** This row ends with k2tog and not k1 as previously.)
Row 26: P13 (15, 17), p2tog, p1 with both strands; turn.

FOOT

Set-up Rnd: Ssk, k6 (7, 8). Pm at center of sole, k7 (8, 9), pick up and knit 7 sts evenly spaced across one side of the heel flap, k28 (30, 32) across instep, pick up and knit 7 sts evenly spaced across other side of heel flap and k7 (8, 9) on sole. The beginning of the rnd is at center of sole.
Foot: Knit 33 (36, 39) rnds on the 56 (60, 64) sts of foot. Divide the sts onto 4 dpn with 14 (15, 16) sts on each needle. Shape toe as follows, with 8 sts decreased on each decrease rnd.
Rnd 1 (decrease rnd): At beginning of each needle: K1, k2tog. At end of each needle: K2tog, k1.
Rnd 2: Knit.
Repeat Rnds 1-2 until 16 (20, 16) sts rem. Cut yarn and draw end through remaining sts. Pull tight and weave in all ends neatly on WS.

FINISHING

Steam press slippers.
Embroider Magnus with duplicate stitch, following the chart. Determine the center of the slipper by folding it flat. Finish by embroidering the green toe tip and then felt the slippers.

Magnus the Garden Mouse was the inspiration for these slippers. We've used the same motif on an iPhone cover. The gardener looked out and discovered the mouse in the potted plants. It was safest to stand on a step-stool.

Embroidery Chart Slipper 1

Center front

Embroidery Chart Slipper 2

Center front

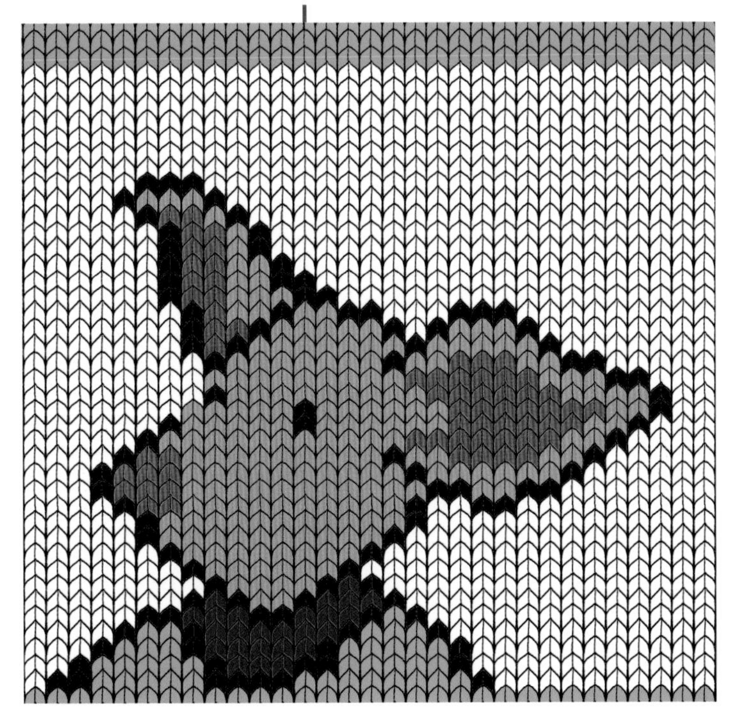

Slippers with crocheted flowers

These slippers feature crocheted flowers that are sewn tightly together for a fine ruched effect.

MATERIALS FOR SLIPPERS

YARN: Rauma Vamsegarn (CYCA #4, worsted/afghan/aran; 100% wool; 91 yd/83 m / 50 g)
3-4 balls Bright Turquoise V76

NEEDLES: U.S. size 8-10 / 5-6 mm: circular and set of 5 dpn

RECOMMENDED GAUGE: 14-16 sts = 4 in / 10 cm

NOTES

Don't forget to alternate two strands of yarn on every stitch throughout.
For additional details about knitting the slippers, refer to Chapter 3, Basic Slippers, pages 15-19.

With one strand of Bright Turquoise and circular, CO 56 (60, 64) sts. Join second strand of Bright Turquoise and knit 10 rows back and forth in garter st, alternating the two strands on every stitch.
Join for the short cuff: Work 28 (30, 32) sts to center back, pm for beginning of rnd, and knit 3 rnds.

HEEL

ROW 1: K14 (15, 16), knitting last st with both strands; turn.
ROW 2: Sl 1, p27 (29, 31), purling last st with both strands; turn.
Work another 11 rows back and forth in stockinette over the 28 (30, 32) heel sts, always slipping the first st.

HEEL TURN

ROW 14: P13 (15, 17), p2tog, p1 with both strands; turn.
ROW 15: K3 (5, 7), k2tog, k1 with both strands; turn.
ROWS 16-23: Continue the same way, working back and forth in stockinette and shaping, with 1 more st before the decrease on each row (the decrease joins the sts before/after the gap).
ROW 24: P12 (14, 16), p2tog, p1 with both strands; turn.
ROW 25: K13 (15, 17), k2tog with both strands; turn.
(**NOTE:** This row ends with k2tog and not k1 as previously.)
ROW 26: P13 (15, 17), p2tog, p1 with both strands; turn.

FOOT

SET-UP RND: Ssk, k6 (7, 8). Pm at center of sole, k7 (8, 9), pick up and knit 7 sts evenly spaced across one side of the heel flap, k28 (30, 32) across instep, pick up and knit 7 sts evenly spaced across other side of heel flap and k7 (8, 9) on sole. The beginning of the rnd is at center of sole.
FOOT: Knit 33 (36, 39) rnds on the 56 (60, 64) sts of foot. Divide the sts onto 4 dpn with 14 (15, 16) sts on each needle. Shape toe as follows, with 8 sts decreased on each decrease rnd.
RND 1 (DECREASE RND): At beginning of each needle: K1, k2tog. At end of each needle: K2tog, k1.
RND 2: Knit.
Repeat Rnds 1-2 until 16 (20, 16) sts rem. Cut yarn and draw end through remaining sts. Pull tight and weave in all ends neatly on WS.

FINISHING

Steam press slippers. Felt the slippers before you embellish them with flowers.

FLOWERS

We used leftover yarns for our flowers. The colors we selected are similar to Rauma Mitu:
Pink 8141
Purple 5090 (a little darker)
Dark Blue 4922
Orange 0784
Yellow 6240
Deep Red 6085 (the closest color in the Mitu range)
Sometimes colors are no longer available, so, in that case, use your imagination and your own choice of colors.

CROCHET HOOK: U.S. size D-3 / 3 mm

FLOWER CENTERS

With Yellow, ch 6 and join into a ring with 1 sl st. Make 6 chain loops around as follows:
1 sc around ring, ch 6, 1 sc around ring; rep * to * 5 more times and end with 1 sl st into 1st ch loop; cut yarn and bring tail through last st and tighten.

FLOWER PETALS

Crochet around each of the 6 chain loops as follows: (1 sc, 2 dc, 5 tr, 2 dc, 1 sc); end rnd with 1 sl st into base of 1st petal. Cut yarn and bring tail through last st and tighten. Make 2 Orange, 4 Dark Blue, 4 Deep Red, 4 Pink, and 4 Purple flowers. Weave in ends and sew flowers into a bouquet. We didn't steam the flowers to keep the fullness.

These slippers were inspired by a Grindley china service from 1930 with the pieces encircled by relief pansies. At first we only had one bowl from Arne's great-grandmother but we've added to our collection by shopping at auctions over the past few years.

Slippers with art deco flowers

MATERIALS

YARN: Rauma Vamsegarn (CYCA #4, worsted/afghan/aran; 100% wool; 91 yd/83 m / 50 g)
3-4 balls Dark Brown Heather V64

NEEDLES: U.S. size 8-10 / 5-6 mm: circular and set of 5 dpn

RECOMMENDED GAUGE: 14-16 sts = 4 in / 10 cm

NOTES

Don't forget to alternate two strands of yarn on every stitch throughout.
For additional details about knitting the slippers, refer to Chapter 3, Basic Slippers, pages 15-19.

With one strand of Dark Brown Heather and circular, CO 56 (60, 64) sts and knit 15 rows back and forth in garter st, alternating the two strands on every stitch.
Join for the short cuff: Work 28 (30, 32) sts to center back, pm for beginning of rnd, and knit 13 rnds.

HEEL

ROW 1: K14 (15, 16), knitting last st with both strands; turn.
ROW 2: Sl 1, p27 (29, 31), purling last st with both strands; turn.
Work another 11 rows back and forth in stockinette over the 28 (30, 32) heel sts, always slipping the first st.

HEEL TURN

ROW 14: P13 (15, 17), p2tog, p1 with both strands; turn.
ROW 15: K3 (5, 7), k2tog, k1 with both strands; turn.
ROWS 16-23: Continue the same way, working back and forth in stockinette and shaping, with 1 more st before the decrease on each row (the decrease joins the sts before/after the gap).
ROW 24: P12 (14, 16), p2tog, p1 with both strands; turn.
ROW 25: K13 (15, 17), k2tog with both strands; turn. (Note: This row ends with k2tog and not k1 as previously.)
ROW 26: P13 (15, 17), p2tog, p1 with both strands; turn.

FOOT

SET-UP RND: Ssk, k6 (7, 8). Pm at center of sole, k7 (8, 9), pick up and knit 7 sts evenly spaced across one side of the heel flap, k28 (30, 32) across instep, pick up and knit 7 sts evenly spaced across other side of heel flap and k7 (8, 9) on sole. The beginning of the rnd is at center of sole.
FOOT: Knit 33 (36, 39) rnds on the 56 (60, 64) sts of foot.
Divide the sts onto 4 dpn with 14 (15, 16) sts on each needle. Shape toe as follows, with 8 sts decreased on each decrease rnd.
RND 1 (DECREASE RND): At beginning of each needle: K1, k2tog. At end of each needle: K2tog, k1.
RND 2: Knit.
Repeat Rnds 1-2 until 16 (20, 16) sts rem. Cut yarn and draw end through remaining sts. Pull tight and weave in all ends neatly on WS.

FINISHING

Steam press and then felt slippers.

FLOWERS AND LEAVES

We used leftover yarns for our flowers and leaves. The colors we selected are similar to Rauma Mitu:
Orange 0784
Yellow 6240
Pink 8141
Green 2196 (darker)
Purple 5090 (darker)
If you use a lot of yarn, you are bound to have the colors you need for some flowers.

CROCHET HOOK: U.S. size D-3 / 3 mm

FLOWERS

Wrap the Yellow yarn around your finger 2-3 times and crochet around the ring at the same time as catching and covering the yarn tail:
RND 1: 1 sc, (ch 3, 1 sc) 6 times (= 6 ch loops).
Cut yarn and bring tail through last st; tighten.
Crochet the petals with Orange, Purple, or Pink as follows:
RND 2: Around each ch loop, work (1 sc, ch 3, 2 tr, ch 3, 1 sl st around loop). End rnd with 1 sl st around last loop.
Cut yarn and fasten off all ends. Steam press flowers gently.

LEAVES

With Green, ch 8.
Work back along the chain, as follows:
2 dc in 3rd ch from hook.
2 tr in 4th ch from hook.
1 dc in 5th ch from hook,
1 dc in 6th ch from hook.
1 sl st in 1st ch (7th ch from hook), ch 3 and 1 sl st into same st as previous sl st.
Now work along opposite side of foundation chain:
1 dc in 6th ch.
1 dc in 5th ch.
2 tr in 4th ch.
1 dc, ch 2 and 1 sl st in 3rd ch.
Cut yarn and pull end through last st; tighten.
Weave in all ends neatly on WS. Gently steam press the leaves.
Arrange the flowers and leaves around each slipper cuff (folding down cuffs). The pair shown is the Medium size. One slipper has 1 Pink, 2 Purple, and 2 Orange flowers, and 8 leaves. Sew flowers on using matching sewing thread.

Slippers bordered with tulips

The motif for these slippers was inspired by a tulip vase that Arne bought for his mother many years ago. The flowers on the slippers are knitted in while the green leaves are embroidered afterwards with duplicate stitch. We used various colors for the inside of each tulip to liven up the flowers.

MATERIALS

YARN

Rauma Vamsegarn (CYCA #4, worsted/afghan/aran; 100% wool; 91 yd/83 m / 50 g)
3-4 balls Taupe V55
1 ball Light Yellow V20
1 ball Red V18
1 ball Spring Green V45
Small amounts of Orange V43, Clover Pink V65, Light Lilac V71, and Deep Rose Pink V44.

NEEDLES: U.S. size 8-10 / 5-6 mm: circular and set of 5 dpn

RECOMMENDED GAUGE: 14-16 sts = 4 in / 10 cm

NOTES

Don't forget to alternate two strands of yarn on every stitch throughout.
For additional details about knitting the slippers, refer to Chapter 3, Basic Slippers, pages 15-19.

With one strand of Yellow and circular, CO 56 (60, 64) sts; join, being careful not to twist cast-on row. Join second strand of Yellow and knit around following the chart, beginning at marker for your size; the first row of the chart = cast-on row. After completing charted rows, continue with two strands of Taupe, working heel as follows:

HEEL

ROW 1: K14 (15, 16), knitting last st with both strands; turn.
ROW 2: Sl 1, p27 (29, 31), purling last st with both strands; turn.
Work another 11 rows back and forth in stockinette over the 28 (30, 32) heel sts, always slipping the first st.

HEEL TURN

ROW 14: P13 (15, 17), p2tog, p1 with both strands; turn.
ROW 15: K3 (5, 7), k2tog, k1 with both strands; turn.
ROWS 16-23: Continue the same way, working back and forth in stockinette and shaping, with 1 more st before the decrease on each row (the decrease joins the sts before/after the gap).
ROW 24: P12 (14, 16), p2tog, p1 with both strands; turn.
ROW 25: K13 (15, 17), k2tog with both strands; turn.
(**NOTE:** This row ends with k2tog and not k1 as previously.)
ROW 26: P13 (15, 17), p2tog, p1 with both strands; turn.

FOOT

SET-UP RND: Ssk, k6 (7, 8). Pm at center of sole, k7 (8, 9), pick up and knit 7 sts evenly spaced across one side of the heel flap, k28 (30, 32) across instep, pick up and knit 7 sts evenly spaced across other side of heel flap and k7 (8, 9) on sole. The beginning of the rnd is at center of sole.
FOOT: Knit 33 (36, 39) rnds on the 56 (60, 64) sts of foot. Divide the sts onto 4 dpn with 14 (15, 16) sts on each needle. Shape toe as follows, with 8 sts decreased on each decrease rnd.
RND 1 (DECREASE RND): At beginning of each needle: K1, k2tog. At end of each needle: K2tog, k1.
RND 2: Knit.
Repeat Rnds 1-2 until 16 (20, 16) sts rem. Cut yarn and draw end through remaining sts. Pull tight and weave in all ends neatly on WS.

FINISHING

Steam press slippers.
Embroider the green leaves and flower details onto the slippers with duplicate stitch.
Steam press embroidery and then felt slippers.

Chart for Tulips

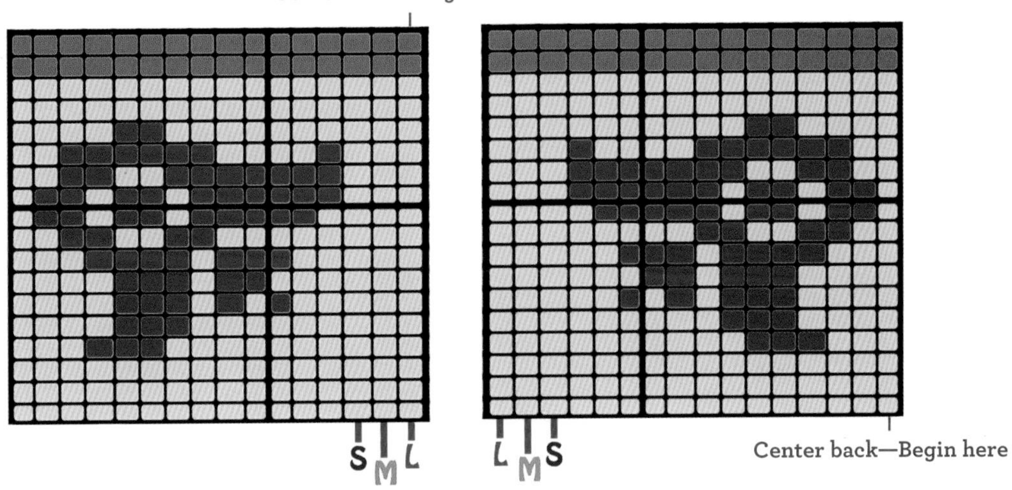

Chart for Embroidered Tulips

Rose slippers

Our rose motifs were inspired by an old pillow embroidered with cross stitch.

MATERIALS

YARN: Rauma Vamsegarn (CYCA #4, worsted/afghan/aran; 100% wool; 91 yd/83 m / 50 g)
3-4 balls Light Lilac V71

EMBROIDERY: small amounts of Clover V65, Red V18, Dark Brown Heather V64, Olive Green V87, Spring Green V45, Pale Pink V66

NEEDLES: U.S. size 8-10 / 5-6 mm: circular and set of 5 dpn

RECOMMENDED GAUGE: 14-16 sts = 4 in / 10 cm

NOTES

Don't forget to alternate two strands of yarn on every stitch throughout.
For additional details about knitting the slippers, refer to Chapter 3, Basic Slippers, pages 15-19.

With one strand of Light Lilac and circular, CO 56 (60, 64) sts; join, being careful not to twist cast-on row. Join second strand of Light Lilac and knit 3 rnds, alternating strands on every stitch.

HEEL

ROW 1: K14 (15, 16), knitting last st with both strands; turn.
ROW 2: Sl 1, p27 (29, 31), purling last st with both strands; turn.
Work another 11 rows back and forth in stockinette over the 28 (30, 32) heel sts, always slipping the first st.

HEEL TURN

ROW 14: P13 (15, 17), p2tog, p1 with both strands; turn.
ROW 15: K3 (5, 7), k2tog, k1 with both strands; turn.
ROWS 16-23: Continue the same way, working back and forth in stockinette and shaping, with 1 more st before the decrease on each row (the decrease joins the sts before/after the gap).
ROW 24: P12 (14, 16), p2tog, p1 with both strands; turn.
ROW 25: K13 (15, 17), k2tog with both strands; turn.
(**NOTE:** This row ends with k2tog and not k1 as previously.)
ROW 26: P13 (15, 17), p2tog, p1 with both strands; turn.

FOOT

SET-UP RND: Ssk, k6 (7, 8). Pm at center of sole, k7 (8, 9), pick up and knit 7 sts evenly spaced across one side of the heel flap, k28 (30, 32) across instep, pick up and knit 7 sts evenly spaced across other side of heel flap and k7 (8, 9) on sole. The beginning of the rnd is at center of sole.
FOOT: Knit 33 (36, 39) rnds on the 56 (60, 64) sts of foot. Divide the sts onto 4 dpn with 14 (15, 16) sts on each needle. Shape toe as follows, with 8 sts decreased on each decrease rnd.
RND 1 (DECREASE RND): At beginning of each needle: K1, k2tog. At end of each needle: K2tog, k1.
RND 2: Knit.
Repeat Rnds 1-2 until 16 (20, 16) sts rem. Cut yarn and draw end through remaining sts. Pull tight and weave in all ends neatly on WS.

FINISHING

Steam press slippers.
Embroider the rose motif onto the slippers with duplicate stitch. The motif is worked over 28 stitches.
Center the motif on each slipper instep or as you like so that it is smooth and balanced.
Steam press the embroidery and then felt slippers.

May fortune's roses
flower along your path
and the butterflies of happiness
flutter over you.

Poem from an old remembrance book

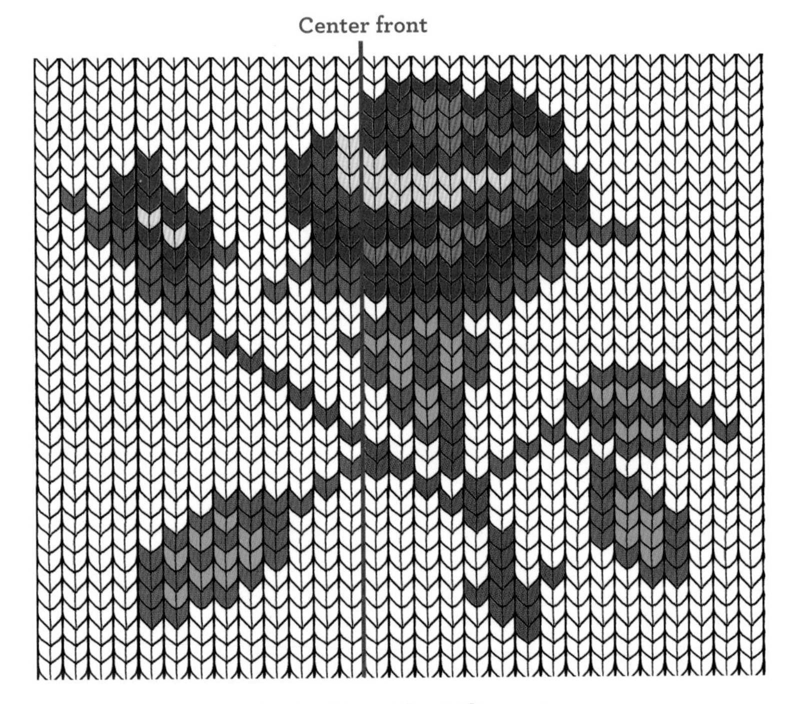

Embroidery Chart Slipper 1

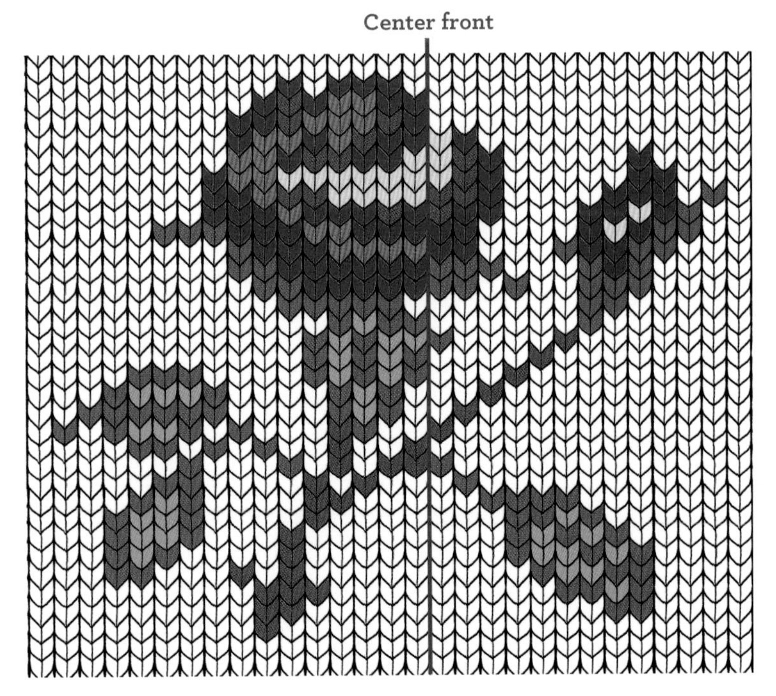

Embroidery Chart Slipper 2

Chapter 8

Rabbits

We certainly couldn't write a book about slippers without the obligatory pair with rabbits and pompoms. In this chapter, you'll find four variations on the theme.

Rabbit and carrot slippers

These slippers feature an embroidered rabbit sitting behind a carrot, so, of course, the slippers must be knitted with orange yarn. The embroidery requires some patience because the area for it is a little tight at the tip of the slipper.

MATERIALS

Yarn: Rauma Vamsegarn (CYCA #4, worsted/afghan/ aran; 100% wool; 91 yd/83 m / 50 g), 3-4 balls Orange V43

Needles: U.S. size 8-10 / 5-6 mm: circular and set of 5 dpn

Recommended Gauge: 14-16 sts = 4 in / 10 cm

Notions:
DMC Embroidery Thread, 4 skeins White (Blanc), 1 skein Red 666, 3 skeins Green 505
Aida 354 waste canvas
sewing needle

NOTES

Don't forget to alternate two strands of yarn on every stitch throughout.
For additional details about knitting the slippers, refer to Chapter 3, Basic Slippers, pages 15-19.

With one strand of Orange and circular, CO 56 (60, 64) sts and then add second strand of Orange. Knit 10 rows back and forth in garter st, alternating the two strands on every stitch.
Join for the short cuff: Work 28 (30, 32) sts to center back, pm for beginning of rnd, and knit 13 rnds.

HEEL

Row 1: K14 (15, 16), knitting last st with both strands; turn.
Row 2: Sl 1, p27 (29, 31), purling last st with both strands; turn.
Work another 11 rows back and forth in stockinette over the 28 (30, 32) heel sts, always slipping the first st.

HEEL TURN

Row 14: P13 (15, 17), p2tog, p1 with both strands; turn.
Row 15: K3 (5, 7), k2tog, k1 with both strands; turn.
Rows 16-23: Continue the same way, working back and forth in stockinette and shaping, with 1 more st before the decrease on each row (the decrease joins the sts before/ after the gap).
Row 24: P12 (14, 16), p2tog, p1 with both strands; turn.
Row 25: K13 (15, 17), k2tog with both strands; turn. (**NOTE:** This row ends with k2tog and not k1 as previously.)
Row 26: P13 (15, 17), p2tog, p1 with both strands; turn.

FOOT

Set-up Rnd: Ssk, k6 (7, 8). Pm at center of sole, k7 (8, 9), pick up and knit 7 sts evenly spaced across one side of the heel flap, k28 (30, 32) across instep, pick up and knit 7 sts evenly spaced across other side of heel flap and k7 (8, 9) on sole. The beginning of the rnd is at center of sole.
Foot: Knit 33 (36, 39) rnds on the 56 (60, 64) sts of foot. Divide the sts onto 4 dpn with 14 (15, 16) sts on each needle. Shape toe as follows, with 8 sts decreased on each decrease rnd.
Rnd 1 (decrease rnd): At beginning of each needle: K1, k2tog. At end of each needle: K2tog, k1.
Rnd 2: Knit.
Repeat Rnds 1-2 until 16 (20, 16) sts rem. Cut yarn and draw end through remaining sts. Pull tight and weave in all ends neatly on WS.

FINISHING

Steam press slippers and then felt slippers.
Center the waste canvas on the slipper, with the edge directly below the split in the collar. Do not divide the plies of the embroidery thread.
Begin the embroidery with the white ear at the center of the motif, with the top of the first cross stitch in the 12th hole from the top of the canvas. Continue working from the chart.
When the embroidery is complete, remove the threads from the canvas. Be careful when removing the threads from the outer edge of the embroidery, because it is easy to pull a little too hard and distort the stitches.

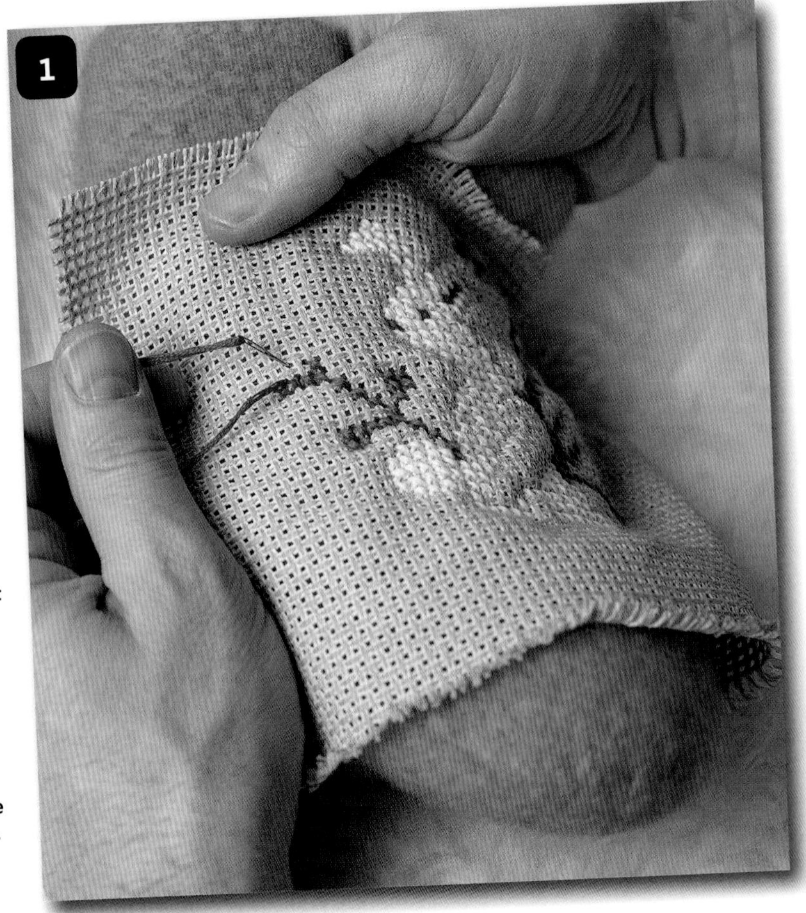

CROSS STITCH

Photo 1: Sew the first stitch on the diagonal from one hole to the second hole on the next row.

Photo 2: When working several crosses in the same color one after the other, sew the first step of each cross at the same time.

Photo 3: Sew the second and last step of the cross on the diagonal on the way back so the threads will cross the same way throughout.

Photo 4: Carefully remove the waste canvas after you've completed all the embroidery.

Embroidery Chart Slipper 1

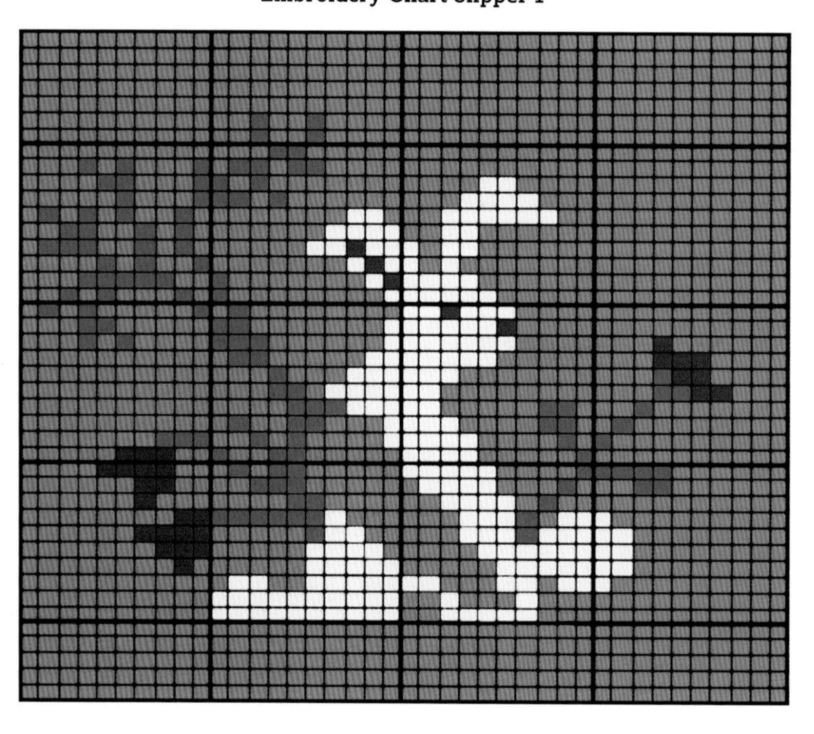

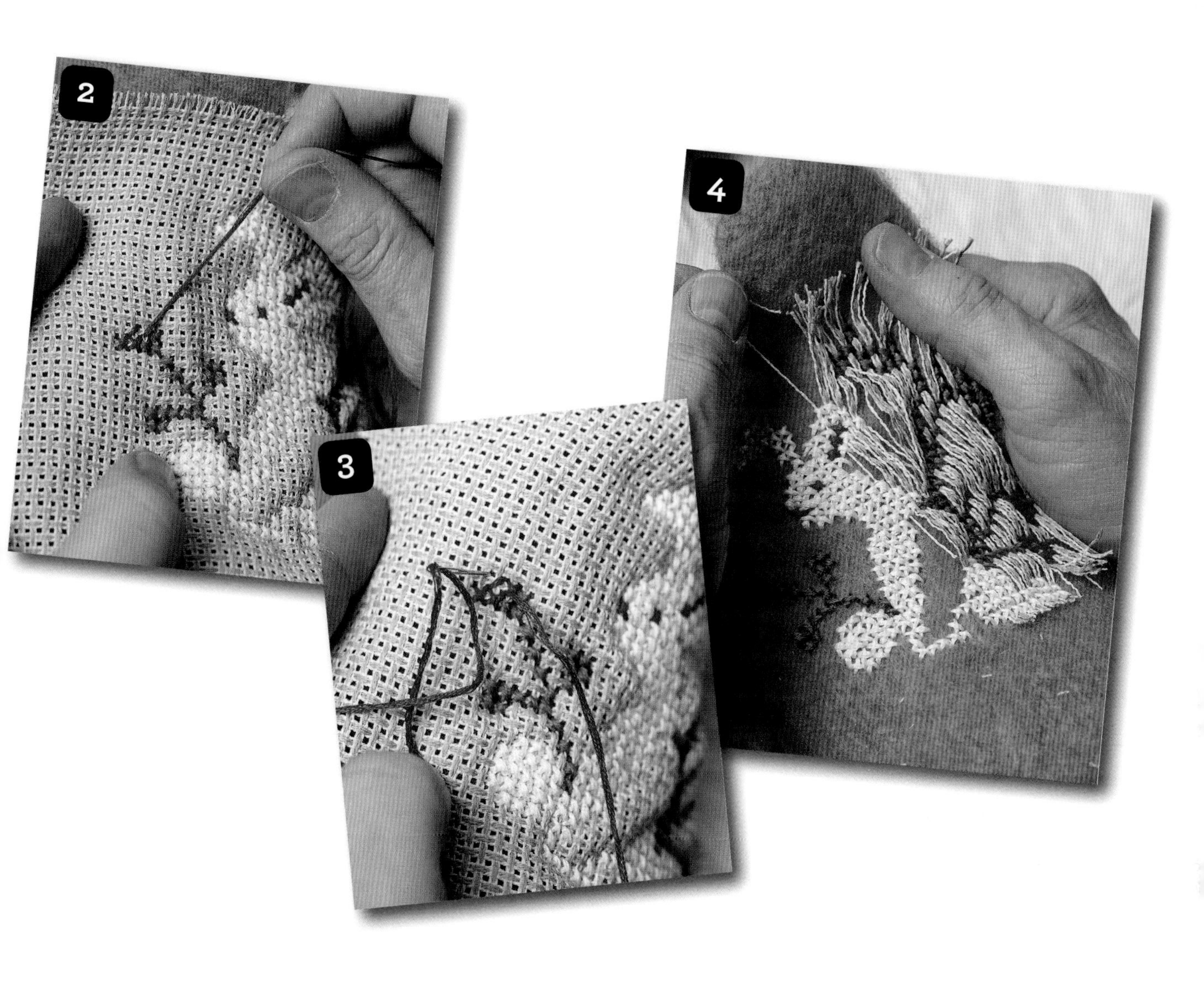

Embroidery Chart Slipper 2

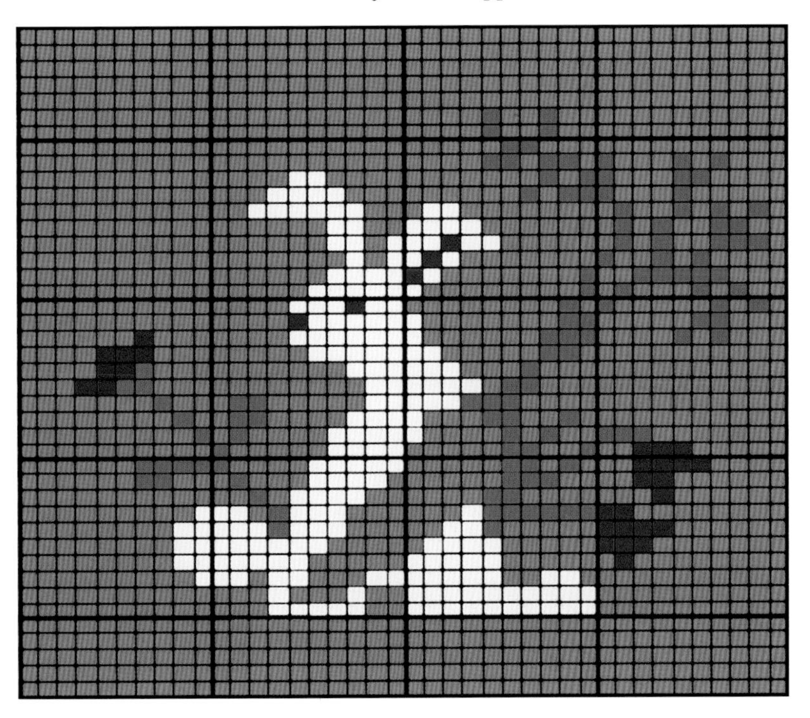

Rabbit slippers with ears

The ultimate rabbit slippers! These slippers should be felted with the ears already attached. The ears will flop differently from one slipper to the next and that's part of their charm.

MATERIALS

Yarn: Rauma Vamsegarn (CYCA #4, worsted/afghan/aran; 100% wool; 91 yd/83 m / 50 g)
3-4 balls Medium Blue V50
1 ball Off-White V01
1 ball Pale Pink V66
Small amounts of Black and Red for the face

Needles: U.S. size 8-10 / 5-6 mm: circular and set of 5 dpn

Crochet Hook: between U.S. size H-8 and J-10 / 5 and 6 mm

Recommended Gauge: 14-16 sts = 4 in / 10 cm

NOTES

Don't forget to alternate two strands of yarn on every stitch throughout.
For additional details about knitting the slippers, refer to Chapter 3, Basic Slippers, pages 15-19.

With one strand of Medium Blue and circular, CO 56 (60, 64) sts; join, being careful not to twist cast-on row. Knit 3 rnds.
Join second strand of Medium Blue and continue on heel, alternating strands on every stitch.

HEEL

Row 1: K14 (15, 16), knitting last st with both strands; turn.
Row 2: Sl 1, p27 (29, 31), purling last st with both strands; turn.
Work another 11 rows back and forth in stockinette over the 28 (30, 32) heel sts, always slipping the first st.

HEEL TURN

Row 14: P13 (15, 17), p2tog, p1 with both strands; turn.
Row 15: K3 (5, 7), k2tog, k1 with both strands; turn.
Rows 16-23: Continue the same way, working back and forth in stockinette and shaping, with 1 more st before the decrease on each row (the decrease joins the sts before/after the gap).
Row 24: P12 (14, 16), p2tog, p1 with both strands; turn.
Row 25: K13 (15, 17), k2tog with both strands; turn. (**NOTE:** This row ends with k2tog and not k1 as previously.)
Row 26: P13 (15, 17), p2tog, p1 with both strands; turn.

FOOT

Set-up Rnd: Ssk, k6 (7, 8). Pm at center of sole, k7 (8, 9), pick up and knit 7 sts evenly spaced across one side of the heel flap, k28 (30, 32) across instep, pick up and knit 7 sts evenly spaced across other side of heel flap and k7 (8, 9) on sole. The beginning of the rnd is at center of sole.
Foot: Knit 33 (36, 39) rnds on the 56 (60, 64) sts of foot. Divide the sts onto 4 dpn with 14 (15, 16) sts on each needle. Shape toe as follows, with 8 sts decreased on each decrease rnd.
Rnd 1 (decrease rnd): At beginning of each needle: K1, k2tog. At end of each needle: K2tog, k1.
Rnd 2: Knit.
Repeat Rnds 1-2 until 16 (20, 16) sts rem. Cut yarn and draw end through remaining sts. Pull tight and weave in all ends neatly on WS.

FINISHING

Steam press slippers.
Embroider the face with duplicate stitch, following the chart.
Steam press the embroidery and then knit the ears.

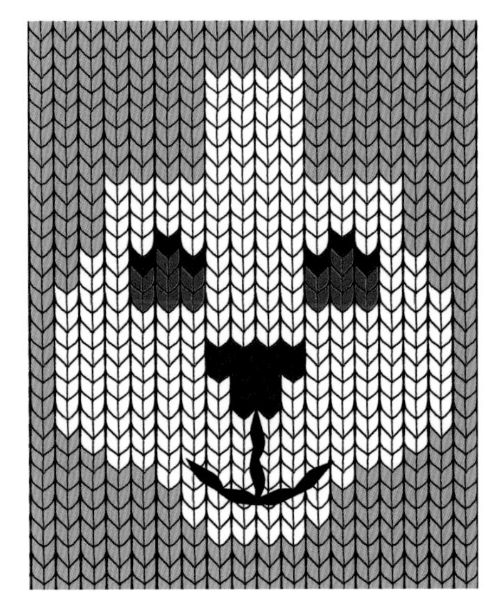

Embroidery

EARS (MAKE 4 ALIKE)

With one strand of Off-White, CO 9 sts and work back and forth in stockinette.
Row 1: P9.

CROCHET THE WHITE AND PINK EAR PIECES TOGETHER

Photos 1-2: Place the ear pieces with WS facing WS and crochet the pieces together with White and single crochet around the outer edge, with the pink side facing you.

Photo 3: Sew the ears with the pink side folding forwards.

Row 2: K9.
Row 3: P9.
Row 4: K9.
Row 5: P9.
Row 6: K1, inc 1 (RLI), k7, inc 1 (LLI), k1.
Row 7: P11.
Row 8: K11.
Row 9: P11.
Row 10: K11.
Row 11: P11.
Row 12: K1, k2tog, k5, k2tog, k1.
Row 13: P9.
Row 14: K9.
Row 15: P9.
Row 16: K9.
Row 17: P9.
Row 18: K1, k2tog, k3, k2tog, k1.
Row 19: P7.
Row 20: K7.
Row 21: P7.
Row 22: K7.
Row 23: P7.
Row 24: K1, k2tog, k1, k2tog, k1.
Row 25: P5.
Row 26: K5.
Row 27: P5.
Row 28: Ssk, k1, k2tog; change to Pink.
Row 29: P3.
Row 30: K3.
Row 31: P3.
Row 32: K3.
Row 33: P3.
Row 34: K1, inc 1 (RLI), k1, inc 1 (LLI), k1.
Row 35: P5.
Row 36: K5.
Row 37: P5.
Row 38: K5.
Row 39: P5.
Row 40: K1, inc 1(RLI), k3, inc 1 (LLI), k1.
Row 41: P7.
Row 42: K7.
Row 43: P7.
Row 44: K7.
Row 45: P7.
Row 46: K1, inc 1 (RLI), k5, inc 1 (LLI), k1.
Row 47: P9.
Row 48: K9.
Row 49: P9.
Row 50: K9.
Row 51: P9.
Row 52: K1, k2tog, k3, k2tog, k1.
Row 53: P7.
Row 54: K7.
Row 55: P7.
Row 56: K7.
Row 57: P7.
BO 7 sts.
Steam press the ears and, with WS facing WS and the pink side facing you, crochet the pieces together with Off-White and slip stitch crochet.
Sew the ears securely to the slippers.
Felt the slippers. When you take the slippers out of the washing machine, fold the ears so that the pink side points forward towards the rabbit's snout. Dry slippers and then make two pompoms 3½ in / 9 cm in diameter. Sew pompoms securely to backs of heels.

In the old days it was common for women to wear slippers in the kitchen. If a married woman was strong, it was said that her husband was “under the slippers”—i.e., “hen-pecked”.

Slippers with embroidered rabbits

Here are some white clog slippers with rabbits embroidered on. The embroidered motif will look better than if it were knitted in because the rabbits are easier to embroider than to knit.

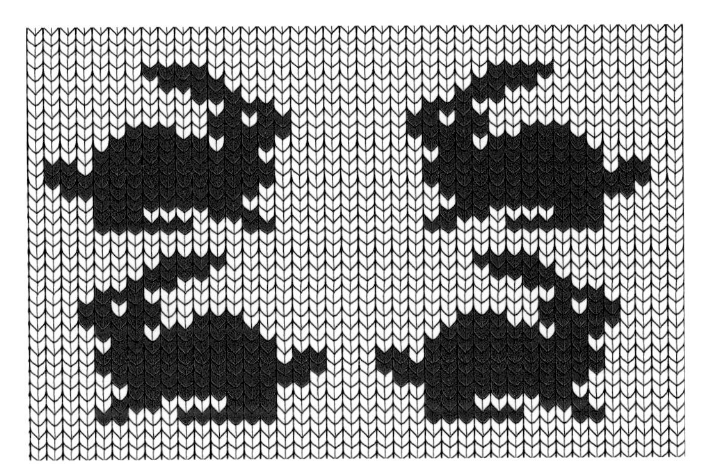

Embroidery Chart

MATERIALS

YARN: Rauma Vamsegarn (CYCA #4, worsted/afghan/ aran; 100% wool; 91 yd/83 m / 50 g)
3-4 balls Off-White V01
1 ball Red Rose V56

NEEDLES: U.S. size 8-10 / 5-6 mm: circular and set of 5 dpn

RECOMMENDED GAUGE: 14-16 sts = 4 in / 10 cm

NOTES

Don't forget to alternate two strands of yarn on every stitch throughout.
For additional details about knitting the slippers, refer to Chapter 3, Basic Slippers, pages 15-19.

With one strand of Off-White and circular, CO 56 (60, 64) sts; join, being careful not to twist cast-on row. Join second strand of Off-White and knit 3 rnds, alternating strands on every stitch.

HEEL

ROW 1: K14 (15, 16), knitting last st with both strands; turn.
ROW 2: Sl 1, p27 (29, 31), purling last st with both strands; turn.
Work another 11 rows back and forth in stockinette over the 28 (30, 32) heel sts, always slipping the first st.

HEEL TURN

ROW 14: P13 (15, 17), p2tog, p1 with both strands; turn.
ROW 15: K3 (5, 7), k2tog, k1 with both strands; turn.
ROWS 16-23: Continue the same way, working back and forth in stockinette and shaping, with 1 more st before the decrease on each row (the decrease joins the sts before/ after the gap).
ROW 24: P12 (14, 16), p2tog, p1 with both strands; turn.
ROW 25: K13 (15, 17), k2tog with both strands; turn.
(**NOTE:** This row ends with k2tog and not k1 as previously.)
ROW 26: P13 (15, 17), p2tog, p1 with both strands; turn.

FOOT

SET-UP RND: Ssk, k6 (7, 8). Pm at center of sole, k7 (8, 9), pick up and knit 7 sts evenly spaced across one side of the heel flap, k28 (30, 32) across instep, pick up and knit 7 sts evenly spaced across other side of heel flap and k7 (8, 9) on sole. The beginning of the rnd is at center of sole.
FOOT: Knit 33 (36, 39) rnds on the 56 (60, 64) sts of foot.
Divide the sts onto 4 dpn with 14 (15, 16) sts on each needle. Shape toe as follows, with 8 sts decreased on each decrease rnd.
RND 1 (DECREASE RND): At beginning of each needle: K1, k2tog. At end of each needle: K2tog, k1.
RND 2: Knit.
Repeat Rnds 1-2 until 16 (20, 16) sts rem. Cut yarn and draw end through remaining sts. Pull tight and weave in all ends neatly on WS.

FINISHING

Steam press slippers.
Embroider the rabbits with duplicate stitch, following the chart. Center the motifs on the insteps of the slippers.
Steam press the embroidery and then felt the slippers.

Slippers with rabbits knitted in

The rabbit motif has long floats between the colors, so we twisted the colors around each other every three stitches. If you want rabbits that fly in all directions, you can mirror-image the patterns when you knit the second slipper. That way, you'll have a left foot and a right foot.

MATERIALS

YARN: Rauma Vamsegarn (CYCA #4, worsted/afghan/aran; 100% wool; 91 yd/83 m / 50 g)
2-3 balls Dark Red V23
1 ball Pale Pink V66

NEEDLES: U.S. size 8-10 / 5-6 mm: circular and set of 5 dpn

RECOMMENDED GAUGE: 14-16 sts = 4 in / 10 cm

NOTES

All sizes begin with the same stitch count so the cuff will be large enough for you to get the slippers on your feet after felting.
Don't forget to alternate two strands of yarn on every stitch throughout.
For additional details about knitting the slippers, refer to Chapter 3, Basic Slippers, pages 15-19.

With one strand of Dark Red and circular, CO 64 sts; join, being careful not to twist cast-on row. Join second strand of Dark Red and knit around, following Rows 2-19 of chart (Row 1 of chart = cast-on row). Alternate 2 strands of the same color on single-color rnds.
On Rnd 20, work alternating the 2 strands of Dark Red, and decrease evenly spaced around as follows:
SIZE S: decrease 8 sts = 56 sts rem
SIZE M: decrease 4 sts = 60 sts rem
SIZE L: decrease 0 sts = 64 sts rem

HEEL

Continue working with two strands of Dark Red as follows:
ROW 1: K14 (15, 16), knitting last st with both strands; turn.
ROW 2: Sl 1, p27 (29, 31), purling last st with both strands; turn.
Work another 11 rows back and forth in stockinette over the 28 (30, 32) heel sts, always slipping the first st.

HEEL TURN

ROW 14: P13 (15, 17), p2tog, p1 with both strands; turn.
ROW 15: K3 (5, 7), k2tog, k1 with both strands; turn.

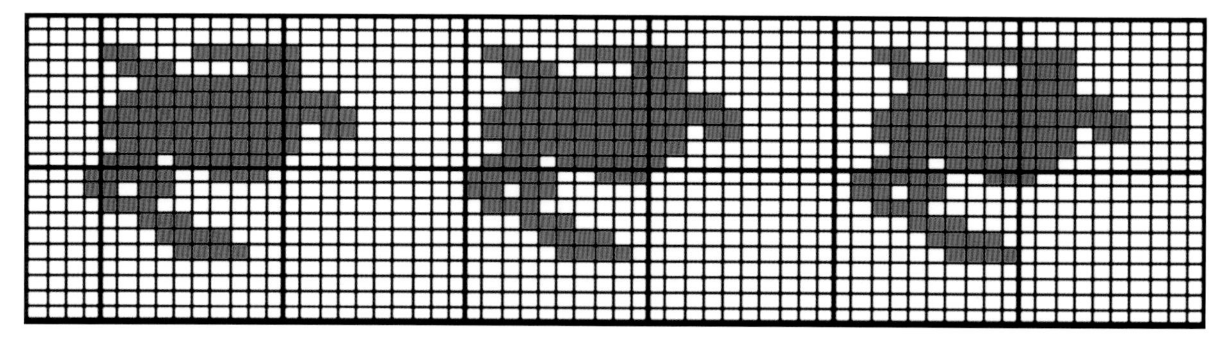

Embroidery Chart for Long Cuff

Rows 16-23: Continue the same way, working back and forth in stockinette and shaping, with 1 more st before the decrease on each row (the decrease joins the sts before/after the gap).
Row 24: P12 (14, 16), p2tog, p1 with both strands; turn.
Row 25: K13 (15, 17), k2tog with both strands; turn.
(**NOTE:** This row ends with k2tog and not k1 as previously.)
Row 26: P13 (15, 17), p2tog, p1 with both strands; turn.

FOOT

Set-up Rnd: Ssk, k6 (7, 8). Pm at center of sole, k7 (8, 9), pick up and knit 7 sts evenly spaced across one side of the heel flap, k28 (30, 32) across instep, pick up and knit 7 sts evenly spaced across other side of heel flap and k7 (8, 9) on sole. The beginning of the rnd is at center of sole.
Foot: Following chart for foot, knit 33 (36, 39) rnds on the 56 (60, 64) sts of foot.
Divide the sts onto 4 dpn with 14 (15, 16) sts on each needle. With Dark Red only, shape toe as follows, with 8 sts decreased on each decrease rnd.
Rnd 1 (decrease rnd): At beginning of each needle: K1, k2tog. At end of each needle: K2tog, k1.
Rnd 2: Knit.
Repeat Rnds 1-2 until 16 (20, 16) sts rem. Cut yarn and draw end through remaining sts. Pull tight and weave in all ends neatly on WS.

FINISHING

Steam press and then felt slippers.

Embroidery Chart for Foot

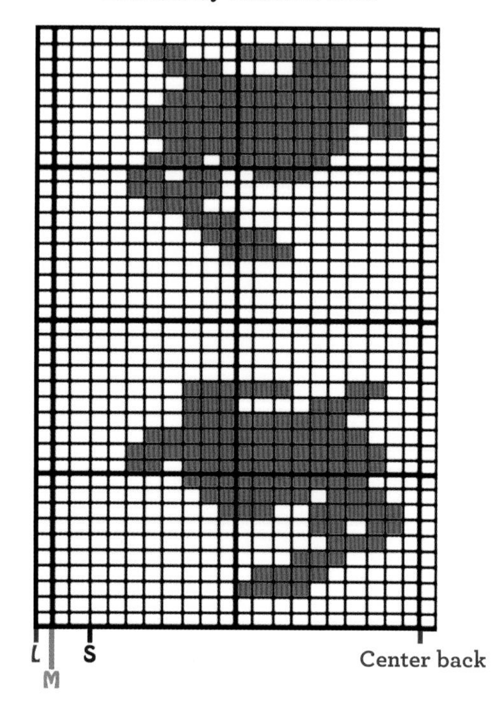

Chapter 9

It's Christmas once again

We, the Christmas ball boys, couldn't write a book without including Christmas. In some ways, Christmas and slippers are connected. Slippers are the ultimate present you can give to someone you care about. You've taken the time to knit them and you want your loved one to have warm feet—that is truly thoughtful!

FLORENCE SARAH WINSHIP

Rudolph slippers

These fun slippers were inspired by the American Christmas song, with a little felted pompom for the red nose. You can form the reindeer antlers with an I-cord.

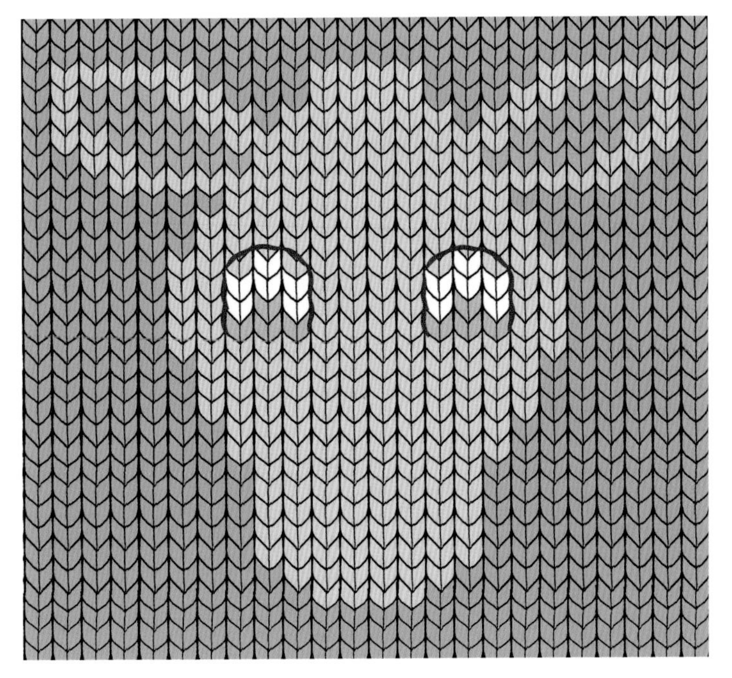

Embroidery Chart

MATERIALS

Yarn: Rauma Vamsegarn (CYCA #4, worsted/afghan/aran; 100% wool; 91 yd/83 m / 50 g)
3-4 balls Lime Green V80
1 ball Red V18
1 ball Light Gray Heather V03
small amounts of Pale Pink V66, Dark Brown Heather V64 (or Black), Medium Blue V50, and White, V00

Needles: U.S. size 8-10 / 5-6 mm: circular and set of 5 dpn

Recommended Gauge: 14-16 sts = 4 in / 10 cm

NOTES

Don't forget to alternate two strands of yarn on every stitch throughout.

For additional details about knitting the slippers, refer to Chapter 3, Basic Slippers, pages 15-19.

With one strand of Lime Green and circular, CO 56 (60, 64) sts; join, being careful not to twist cast-on row. Join second strand of Lime Green and knit 15 rnds, alternating strands on every stitch.

HEEL

Row 1: K14 (15, 16), knitting last st with both strands; turn.
Row 2: Sl 1, p27 (29, 31), purling last st with both strands; turn.
Work another 11 rows back and forth in stockinette over the 28 (30, 32) heel sts, always slipping the first st.

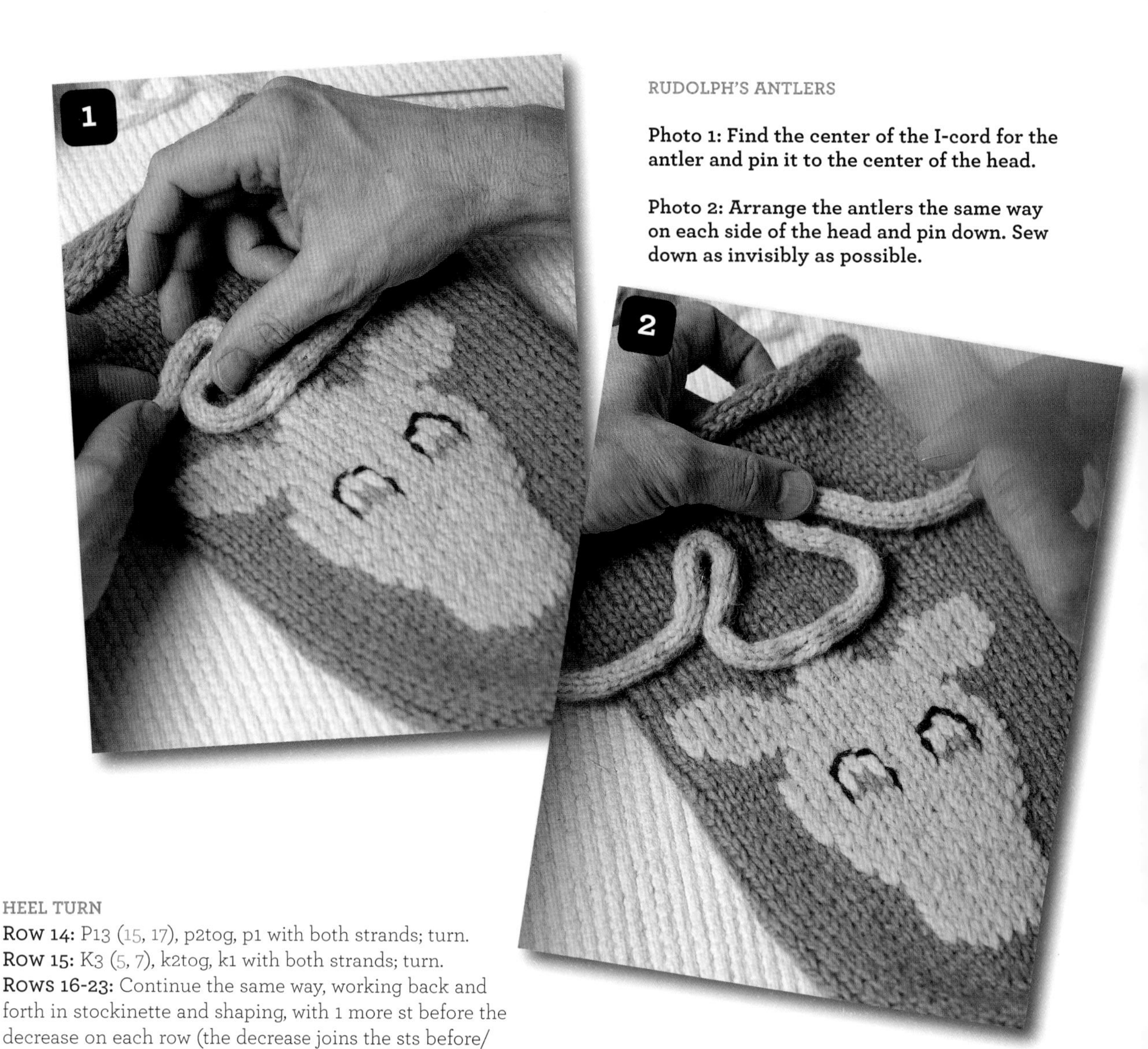

RUDOLPH'S ANTLERS

Photo 1: Find the center of the I-cord for the antler and pin it to the center of the head.

Photo 2: Arrange the antlers the same way on each side of the head and pin down. Sew down as invisibly as possible.

HEEL TURN

Row 14: P13 (15, 17), p2tog, p1 with both strands; turn.
Row 15: K3 (5, 7), k2tog, k1 with both strands; turn.
Rows 16-23: Continue the same way, working back and forth in stockinette and shaping, with 1 more st before the decrease on each row (the decrease joins the sts before/after the gap).
Row 24: P12 (14, 16), p2tog, p1 with both strands; turn.
Row 25: K13 (15, 17), k2tog with both strands; turn. (**NOTE:** This row ends with k2tog and not k1 as previously.)
Row 26: P13 (15, 17), p2tog, p1 with both strands; turn.

FOOT

Set-up Rnd: Ssk, k6 (7, 8). Pm at center of sole, k7 (8, 9), pick up and knit 7 sts evenly spaced across one side of the heel flap, k28 (30, 32) across instep, pick up and knit 7 sts evenly spaced across other side of heel flap and k7 (8, 9) on sole. The beginning of the rnd is at center of sole.
Foot: Knit 33 (36, 39) rnds on the 56 (60, 64) sts of foot. Divide the sts onto 4 dpn with 14 (15, 16) sts on each needle. Shape toe as follows, with 8 sts decreased on each decrease rnd.
Rnd 1 (decrease rnd): At beginning of each needle: K1, k2tog. At end of each needle: K2tog, k1.
Rnd 2: Knit.
Repeat Rnds 1-2 until 16 (20, 16) sts rem. Cut yarn and draw end through remaining sts. Pull tight and weave in all ends neatly on WS.

FINISHING

Steam press slippers.
Embroider the charted motif with duplicate stitch, using Light Gray Heather, Pale Pink, Medium Blue, and White. Edge the eyes between the White and Light Gray Heather areas, using Dark Brown Heather (or Black) and back-stitch.
Steam press the embroidery.

Antlers: Knit 2 I-cords, each about 27½ in / 70 cm long. Shape and attach the antlers as described above. Use a knitting mill for the cords or hand knit them.
I-Cord: With white and dpn, CO 5 sts. Knit across and then *slide sts to front of dpn. Bring yarn around back and k5*. Rep from * to * until cord is desired length. Cut yarn and bring end through sts; tighten and weave in end to WS.

Make two pompoms 2¼ in / 5.5 cm in diameter.

Felt the slippers and pompoms at the same time. Sew on pompoms for the red nose after felting is complete.

For the coziest Christmas evening with the entire family, make sure that each of the guests receives a pair of homemade slippers when they arrive.

OFF = ON

Slippers with embroidered Christmas balls

Classic Arne & Carlos Christmas balls can now be embroidered onto slippers. Use the suggestions in the chart below or design your own.

MATERIALS

YARN: Rauma Vamsegarn (CYCA #4, worsted/afghan/aran; 100% wool; 91 yd/83 m / 50 g)
3-4 balls Spring Green V45
1 ball Off-White V01
1 ball Red V43

NEEDLES: U.S. size 8-10 / 5-6 mm: circular and set of 5 dpn
CROCHET HOOK: between U.S. size H-8 and J-10 / 5 and 6 mm

RECOMMENDED GAUGE: 14-16 sts = 4 in / 10 cm

NOTES

Don't forget to alternate two strands of yarn on every stitch throughout.

For additional details about knitting the slippers, refer to Chapter 3, Basic Slippers, pages 15-19.

With one strand of Red and circular, CO 56 (60, 64) sts; join, being careful not to twist cast-on row. Join second strand of Red and knit 1 rnd, alternating strands on every stitch. Change to two strands of Spring Green and knit 3 rnds.

HEEL

ROW 1: K14 (15, 16), knitting last st with both strands; turn.
ROW 2: Sl 1, p27 (29, 31), purling last st with both strands; turn.
Work another 11 rows back and forth in stockinette over the 28 (30, 32) heel sts, always slipping the first st.

Diagram

Last rnd size L
Last rnd size M
Last rnd size S

X X X
Center back
S M L

HEEL TURN

Row 14: P13 (15, 17), p2tog, p1 with both strands; turn.
Row 15: K3 (5, 7), k2tog, k1 with both strands; turn.
Rows 16-23: Continue the same way, working back and forth in stockinette and shaping, with 1 more st before the decrease on each row (the decrease joins the sts before/after the gap).
Row 24: P12 (14, 16), p2tog, p1 with both strands; turn.
Row 25: K13 (15, 17), k2tog with both strands; turn. (**NOTE:** This row ends with k2tog and not k1 as previously.)
Row 26: P13 (15, 17), p2tog, p1 with both strands; turn.

FOOT

Set-up Rnd: Ssk, k6 (7, 8). Pm at center of sole, k7 (8, 9), pick up and knit 7 sts evenly spaced across one side of the heel flap, k28 (30, 32) across instep, pick up and knit 7 sts evenly spaced across other side of heel flap and k7 (8, 9) on sole. The beginning of the rnd is at center of sole.
Foot: Following the chart, knit 33 (36, 39) rnds on the 56 (60, 64) sts of foot.
Divide the sts onto 4 dpn with 14 (15, 16) sts on each needle. With Spring Green only, shape toe as follows, with 8 sts decreased on each decrease rnd.
Rnd 1 (decrease rnd): At beginning of each needle: K1, k2tog. At end of each needle: K2tog, k1.
Rnd 2: Knit.
Repeat Rnds 1-2 until 16 (20, 16) sts rem. Cut yarn and draw end through remaining sts. Pull tight and weave in all ends neatly on WS.

FINISHING

Steam press slippers.
Embroider in Red for the ornaments with duplicate stitch, following the chart. Steam press embroidery and then felt slippers.

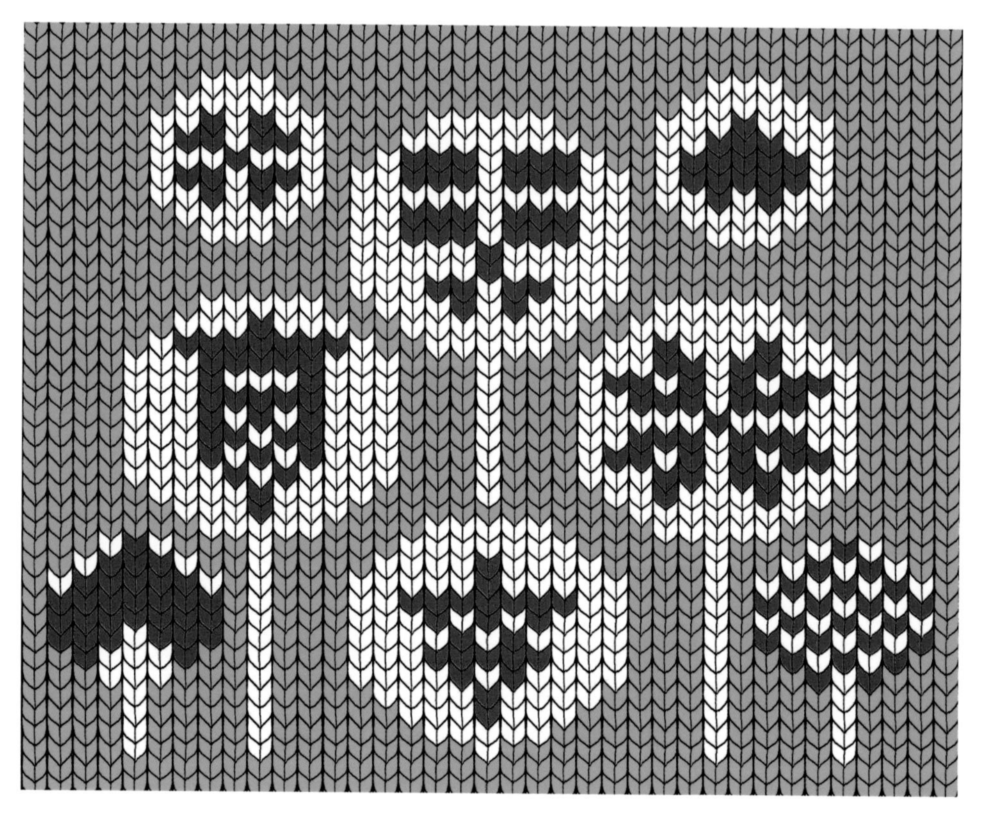

Embroidery Chart

Christmas stockings

These slippers feature a Christmas tree with ornaments embroidered on with red duplicate stitch, while the presents have white embroidery.

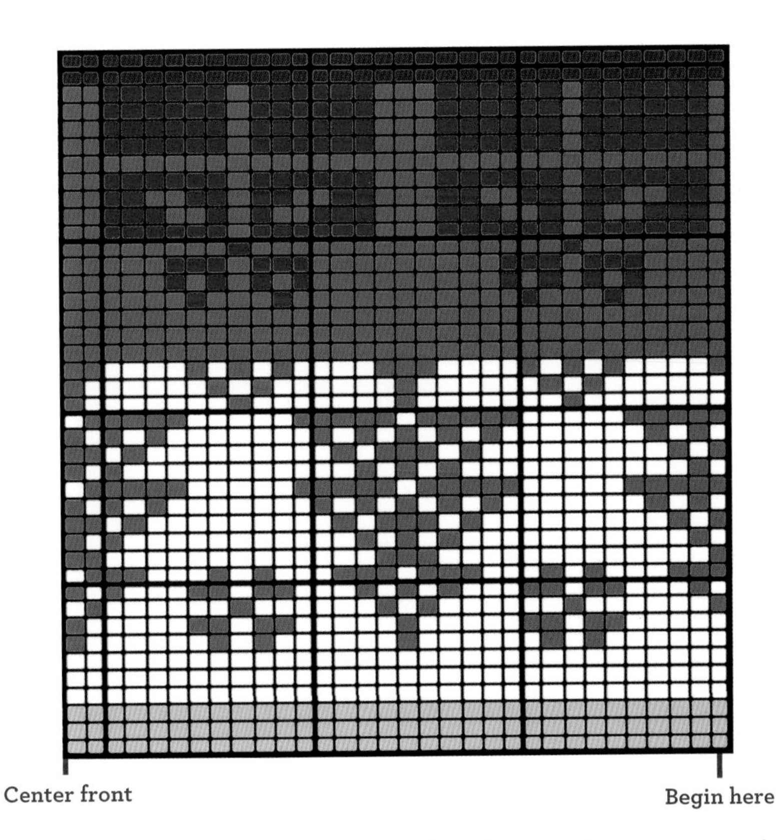

Chart for Long Cuff

MATERIALS

YARN: Rauma Vamsegarn (CYCA #4, worsted/afghan/aran; 100% wool; 91 yd/83 m / 50 g)
3-4 balls Dark Brown Heather V64
1 ball Bright Yellow V26
1 ball Off-White V01
1 ball Dark Green V34
1 ball Red V18

NEEDLES: U.S. size 8-10 / 5-6 mm: circular and set of 5 dpn

RECOMMENDED GAUGE: 14-16 sts = 4 in / 10 cm

NOTES

All sizes begin with the same stitch count so the cuff will be large enough for you to get the slippers on your feet after felting.

Don't forget to alternate two strands of yarn on every stitch throughout.
For additional details about knitting the slippers, refer to Chapter 3, Basic Slippers, pages 15-19.

With one strand of Bright Yellow and circular, CO 64 sts; join, being careful not to twist cast-on row. Join second strand of Bright Yellow and knit around, following chart (Row 1 of chart = cast-on row) until 2 rnds remain. Alternate 2 strands of the same color on single-color rnds. If there is a long float between colors, twist the colors around each other every 3 or 4 sts.
On second-to-last rnd, knit, alternating the 2 strands of Dark Brown Heather, and, on last rnd, decrease evenly spaced around as follows:
SIZE S: decrease 8 sts = 56 sts rem
SIZE M: decrease 4 sts = 60 sts rem
SIZE L: decrease 0 sts = 64 sts rem

Christmas Tree Embroidery Chart

HEEL

Continue working with two strands of Dark Brown Heather as follows:

Row 1: K14 (15, 16), knitting last st with both strands; turn.

Row 2: Sl 1, p27 (29, 31), purling last st with both strands; turn.

Work another 11 rows back and forth in stockinette over the 28 (30, 32) heel sts, always slipping the first st.

HEEL TURN

Row 14: P13 (15, 17), p2tog, p1 with both strands; turn.

Row 15: K3 (5, 7), k2tog, k1 with both strands; turn.

Rows 16-23: Continue the same way, working back and forth in stockinette and shaping, with 1 more st before the decrease on each row (the decrease joins the sts before/after the gap).

Row 24: P12 (14, 16), p2tog, p1 with both strands; turn.

Row 25: K13 (15, 17), k2tog with both strands; turn. (**NOTE:** This row ends with k2tog and not k1 as previously.)

Row 26: P13 (15, 17), p2tog, p1 with both strands; turn.

FOOT

Set-up Rnd: Ssk, k6 (7, 8). Pm at center of sole, k7 (8, 9), pick up and knit 7 sts evenly spaced across one side of the heel flap, k28 (30, 32) across instep, pick up and knit 7 sts evenly spaced across other side of heel flap and k7 (8, 9) on sole. The beginning of the rnd is at center of sole.

Foot: Knit 33 (36, 39) rnds on the 56 (60, 64) sts of foot. Divide the sts onto 4 dpn with 14 (15, 16) sts on each needle. Shape toe as follows, with 8 sts decreased on each decrease rnd.

Rnd 1 (decrease rnd): At beginning of each needle: K1, k2tog. At end of each needle: K2tog, k1.

Rnd 2: Knit.

Repeat Rnds 1-2 until 16 (20, 16) sts rem. Cut yarn and draw end through remaining sts. Pull tight and weave in all ends neatly on WS.

FINISHING

Steam press slippers.

With Off-White and Red yarns, follow the charts to embroider the tree decoration and gifts onto slippers. Steam press embroidery and then felt slippers.

Embroidery Chart for Gifts

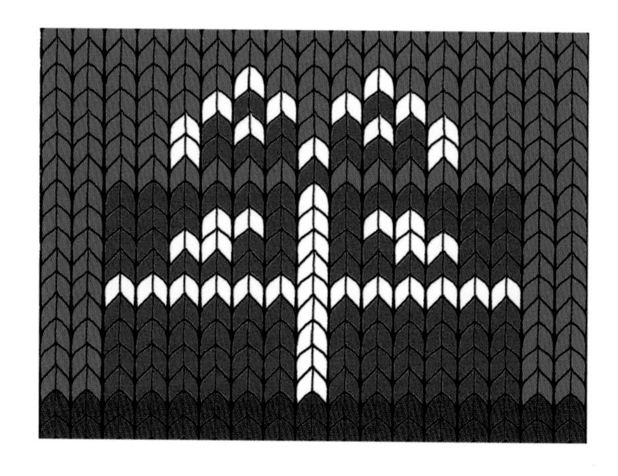

"See the Christmas elf," said the littlest boy. "He has made slippers while we were sleeping, Father."

Mistletoe slippers

If you haven't hung the mistletoe this year, you can always put on these slippers—maybe you'll even get a kiss!

MATERIALS

YARN: Rauma Vamsegarn (CYCA #4, worsted/afghan/aran; 100% wool; 91 yd/83 m / 50 g)
3-4 balls Gold V46
1 ball Light Gray Heather V03
1 ball Evergreen V88
1 ball Red V18

NEEDLES: U.S. size 8-10 / 5-6 mm: circular and set of 5 dpn

RECOMMENDED GAUGE: 14-16 sts = 4 in / 10 cm

NOTES

All sizes begin with the same stitch count so the cuff will be large enough for you to get the slippers on your feet after felting.
Don't forget to alternate two strands of yarn on every stitch throughout.
For additional details about knitting the slippers, refer to Chapter 3, Basic Slippers, pages 15-19.

With one strand of Gold and circular, CO 64 sts; join, being careful not to twist cast-on row. Join second strand of Gold and knit around, following chart (Row 1 of chart = cast-on row) until 1 rnd remains. Alternate 2 strands of the same color on single-color rnds. If there is a long float between colors, twist the colors around each other every 3 or 4 sts.
On last rnd, decrease evenly spaced around as follows:
SIZE S: decrease 8 sts = 56 sts rem
SIZE M: decrease 4 sts = 60 sts rem
SIZE L: decrease 0 sts = 64 sts rem

HEEL

Cut other colors and work rest of slipper with Gold as follows:
ROW 1: K14 (15, 16), knitting last st with both strands; turn.
ROW 2: Sl 1, p27 (29, 31), purling last st with both strands; turn.

Chart for Long Cuff

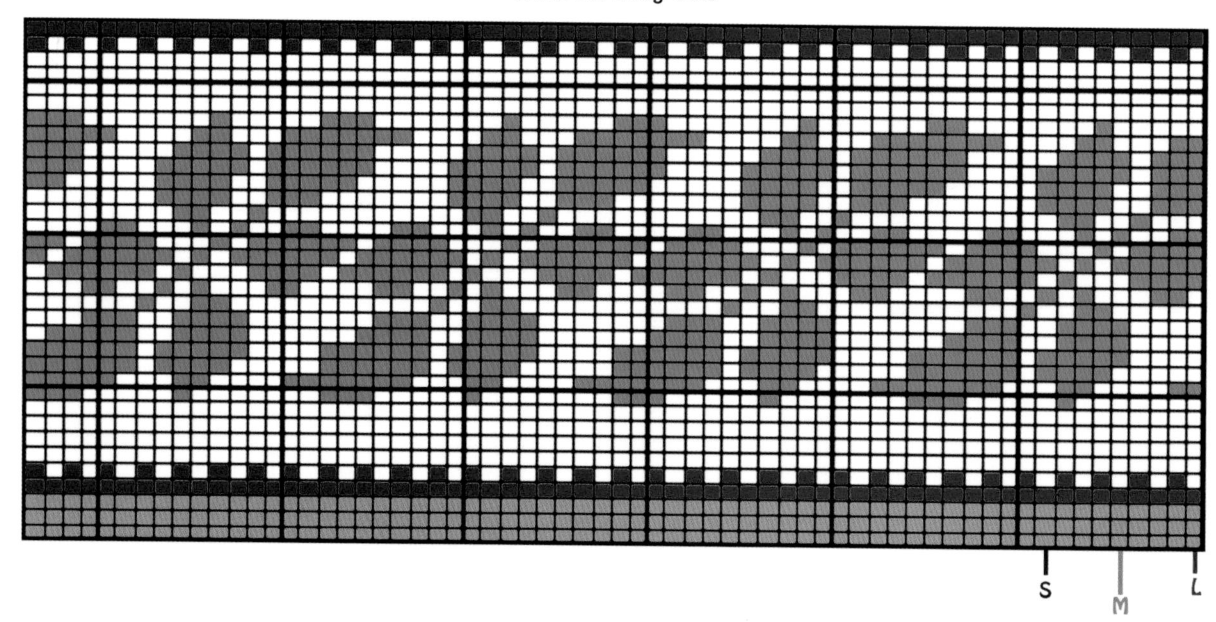

Bonne Année

Embroidery Chart

Work another 11 rows back and forth in stockinette over the 28 (30, 32) heel sts, always slipping the first st.

HEEL TURN

Row 14: P13 (15, 17), p2tog, p1 with both strands; turn.
Row 15: K3 (5, 7), k2tog, k1 with both strands; turn.
Rows 16-23: Continue the same way, working back and forth in stockinette and shaping, with 1 more st before the decrease on each row (the decrease joins the sts before/after the gap).
Row 24: P12 (14, 16), p2tog, p1 with both strands; turn.
Row 25: K13 (15, 17), k2tog with both strands; turn. (**NOTE:** This row ends with k2tog and not k1 as previously.)
Row 26: P13 (15, 17), p2tog, p1 with both strands; turn.

FOOT

Set-up Rnd: Ssk, k6 (7, 8). Pm at center of sole, k7 (8, 9), pick up and knit 7 sts evenly spaced across one side of the heel flap, k28 (30, 32) across instep, pick up and knit 7 sts evenly spaced across other side of heel flap and k7 (8, 9) on sole. The beginning of the rnd is at center of sole.
Foot: Knit 33 (36, 39) rnds on the 56 (60, 64) sts of foot. Divide the sts onto 4 dpn with 14 (15, 16) sts on each needle. Shape toe as follows, with 8 sts decreased on each decrease rnd.
Rnd 1 (decrease rnd): At beginning of each needle: K1, k2tog. At end of each needle: K2tog, k1.
Rnd 2: Knit.
Repeat Rnds 1-2 until 16 (20, 16) sts rem. Cut yarn and draw end through remaining sts. Pull tight and weave in all ends neatly on WS.

FINISHING

Steam press slippers.
Follow the chart to embroider red stitches with duplicate st.
Steam press embroidery and then felt slippers.

References:

Blicher, Steen Steensen. *Fortellinger fra heden—Hosekremmeren* [*Tales from the Heath Lands: The Stocking Peddlers*]. Oslo, Norway: Solum 1976.

Haugen, Anny. *Sami husflid i Finnmark* [*Sami Crafts in Finnmark*]. Oslo, Norway: Landbruksforlaget, 1987.

Kelton, Elmer. *The Art of James Bama*. New York: Bantam Books, 1992.

Taylor, Colin R. *The Native Americans*. London: Tiger Books International, 1995.

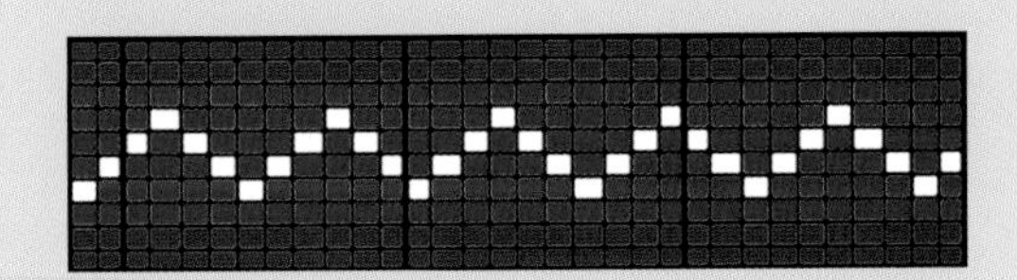

Resources:

Rauma Garn, *Vamsegarn and Mitu:* www.raumaull.no; in U.S.: www.nordicfiberarts.com

Schachenmeyr, *Wash+Filz-it!*: www.coatscrafts.com

DMC, embroidery thread: www.dmcthreads.com

Clover Pompom maker, item 3126: available in most craft and hobby stores

Aida waste canvas: permin.dk or local needlecraft shop

Beads, knitting mill, and liquid latex: available in most craft and hobby stores

Regia ABS Latex for slipper soles: www.coatscrafts.com

Pattern for Magnus the Garden Mouse shown in chapter 7, The Terrace: see Arne & Carlos, *Knit-and-Crochet Garden: Bring a Little Outside In: 36 Projects Inspired by Flowers, Butterflies, Birds, and Bees.* North Pomfret, Vermont: Trafalgar Square Books, 2013. Tunbridge Wells, Kent, Search Press, 2013.

Pattern for the Easter Bunny shown in chapter 8, Rabbits: see Arne & Carlos, *Easter Knits: Eggs, Bunnies, and Chicks—with a Fabulous Twist.* North Pomfret, Vermont: Trafalgar Square Books, 2012. Tunbridge Wells, Kent, Search Press, 2012.

Pattern for Arne and Carlos dolls shown in chapter 9, It's Christmas time again: see Arne & Carlos, *Knitted Dolls: Handmade Toys with a Designer Wardrobe: Knitting Fun for the Child in All of Us.* North Pomfret, Vermont: Trafalgar Square Books, 2011. Tunbridge Wells, Kent, Search Press, 2011.

SVAR: NORGES NORDLIGSTE STED ER
SØRLIGSTE STED ER LINDESNES.